13
MISTAKES INVESTORS CAN AVOID

Master the Art of Mutual Fund Investment
with In-Depth
Self-Evaluations

JAYESH CHOPADE

ISBN: 9798877347373

CONTENT:

PREFACE

Welcome to "13 Mistakes Investors Can Avoid." This book is for anyone who wants to learn about mutual funds and avoid common mistakes that people make when investing in them.

Many people want to invest their money to grow their savings, but knowing the best way to do this is not always easy. Mutual funds can be a great choice, but there are many things to consider when choosing the right one. People often make mistakes without realizing it, which can cost them money.

In this book, I've compiled a list of 100 mistakes people often make. I'll explain each in simple words and show you how to avoid making these mistakes yourself. This book isn't just about what can go wrong; it's also about helping you make smart choices with your money.

Whether you're new to investing or have been doing it for a while, this book can help you. By understanding these common mistakes, you can make better decisions and feel more confident about your investments.

In closing, remember that every investment journey is unique, and so are the challenges and opportunities it presents. May this book serve as a beacon, guiding you through the complex yet rewarding world of mutual funds.

Happy Investing!

Jayesh Chopade

INTRODUCTION

One sunny afternoon, I caught up with my old friend, Dave, at our favorite coffee shop. As we sipped our lattes, our chat quickly turned to our favorite topic: investing. But Dave seemed down. He told me he was moving all his money into a Fixed Deposit. I was surprised and asked him why.

Turns out, Dave had a rough time with his mutual fund investments. He lost quite a bit of money. Curious, I asked him how he chose his mutual funds and what his strategy was. Dave's answers were shocking. He had made some really basic mistakes.

Dave had just picked the funds that were doing well last year, thinking they would do great this year too. He didn't look at the fees or think about how the funds fit with his other investments. And when the market dipped a little, he got scared and sold his shares at a loss.

Hearing this, I realized something. A lot of people, just like Dave, don't know how to pick mutual funds.

They make simple mistakes without even realizing it.

That evening, as I walked home, an idea started to form in my mind. What if I wrote a book to help people like Dave? I could talk about these common mistakes and how to avoid them.

So, I started writing. The book, called "13 Mistakes Investors Can Avoid " is all about the 13 mistakes people often make with mutual funds. Each mistake is a chapter, filled with easy-to-understand explanations, real stories like Dave's, and tips to do better.

This isn't just a book with a list of don'ts. It's a collection of stories and lessons, making learning about mutual funds fun and simple. Whether you're new to investing or you've had a few bumps along the way, this book is for you.

"13 Mistakes Investors Can Avoid" is more than just a guide; it's like a chat with a friend over coffee, helping you learn from other's mistakes. So, grab a cup of coffee, settle into a cozy chair, and join me on this journey to smarter investing in mutual funds.

WHAT IS A MUTUAL FUND?

Let's start by learning what a mutual fund is and why it's often a better choice to invest in one instead of other options.

Imagine a mutual fund as a large pot of money. Lots of different people add their money to this pot. Now, each person can't buy a lot of different stocks or bonds with their money alone. But when everyone's money is put together in this pot, it becomes a lot.

A person called a fund manager is in charge of this pot. They are like the chef in a big kitchen. Just like a chef decides what ingredients to put in a soup, the fund manager decides what stocks or bonds to buy with the money. The fund manager is experienced and knows a lot about the stock market and investing.

When the fund manager buys stocks, they are buying small pieces of different companies. And when they buy bonds, they are lending money to companies or governments, which they will get back with interest.

All the people who put their money in the pot own a share of this mix of stocks and bonds. This means if the value of these stocks and bonds goes up, everyone's share becomes more valuable. But if the value goes down, then everyone's share is worth less.

The good thing about mutual funds is that they let you own a small part of many investments. If you had to buy all these stocks and bonds alone, it would cost a lot of money. But by joining together with others in a mutual fund, you can be a part of bigger investments with less money.

This is the basic idea of a mutual fund. It's a way for lots of people to invest their money together and have a professional manage it for them.

WHY INVEST IN MUTUAL FUNDS?

Expert Management: The biggest plus of a mutual fund is that you have a professional manager making investment decisions for you. It's like having a personal investment coach who takes care of your money.

Diversification: When you invest in a mutual fund, your money gets spread out across many different investments. This is called diversification. It's like not putting all your eggs in one basket. If one investment doesn't do well, others might do better, which can help reduce your risk.

Accessibility: Mutual funds are easy to invest in. You don't need a lot of money to get started, and you can often buy and sell your shares of the fund easily.

Variety: There are tons of mutual funds out there, each with its own strategy and focus. Whether you like to play it safe or take risks, there's probably a mutual fund that fits your style.

Economies of Scale: Because mutual funds pool money from many investors, they can invest in ways smaller investors can't. This often means lower costs or access to investments you might not be able to afford on your own.

Transparency and Regulation: Mutual funds are regulated, which means they have to follow strict rules and be transparent about what they're doing with their money.

Compared to Other Options:

Stocks: If you buy stocks, you're buying a piece of one company. If that company does well, you do well. But if it doesn't, you might lose money. Mutual funds spread the risk by investing in many different stocks (and/or other things).

Bonds: Buying a bond means you're lending money to a company or government. Bonds are generally safer than stocks, but they might not make as much money. Mutual funds often mix stocks and bonds to balance risk and return.

Savings Accounts: These are super safe, but they don't grow much. Mutual funds might have more risk, but they also have the potential for more growth.

In short, mutual funds offer a balance of professional management, diversification, and potential for higher returns, making them a preferred choice for many investors, especially those who might not have the time or expertise to manage their own investments.

Imagine you're at a party, and everyone's talking about investing in mutual funds. It's like everyone's jumping into a pool, but they're all wearing blindfolds! I was at such a gathering recently, and what I heard was pretty surprising.

Some folks were just following the crowd, investing because their friends did or because a social media guru said so. It's like picking a random dish from a menu just because the person at the next table ordered it. Others were investing only to save on taxes, like buying a ticket to a random movie just to use a discount coupon.

Then there were those who didn't really understand what they were getting into. They saw mutual funds like magic pots, thinking any fund they pick will automatically grow money. It's like planting any seed and expecting a rose garden without knowing what the seeds will grow into!

Many didn't consider if the investment was too risky for them, like riding a roller coaster without checking how scary it is. Only a handful of people actually took the time to study different mutual funds and their managers, like chefs tasting and choosing the right ingredients for a recipe.
After chatting with a bunch of people, it hit me. Most people keep making the same simple mistakes over

and over when choosing mutual funds. In my book, I've jotted down 101 of these common blunders. It's like a guide to help you navigate through the maze of mutual fund investing without tripping over these hurdles.

So, if you're thinking about growing your money with mutual funds, this book is like a map. It'll help you steer clear of these pitfalls and make smarter investment choices. Let's dive into the world of mutual funds with open eyes, not blindfolds!

Let's start with mistakes that investors might encounter. I have grouped them into categories.

PART I:
FUNDAMENTALS OF MUTUAL FUND INVESTING

1.
SET CLEAR INVESTMENT GOALS

It means knowing exactly what you want to achieve with your money when you invest it. Think of it like planning a road trip. Before you start driving, you need to know where you're going. Are you heading to the beach, a mountain cabin, or a city break? Each destination requires different preparations and routes.

Similarly, with investing, your goals are your destination. Here are a few examples:
Retirement: Maybe you're saving for the day when you can stop working. You need to figure out how much money you'll need to live comfortably and how long you have to save it.

Buying a Home: If you plan to buy a house, you need to know how much you need for the down payment and when you plan to buy it.

Education: Perhaps you're saving for your kids' college. You'll need to consider how much tuition might cost in the future and how many years until they start college.

Travel or Big Purchases: Maybe you're saving for a dream vacation or a new car. You need to know how much it will cost and when you plan to make the purchase.

Once you know your goals, you can plan your investment strategy:
Timeframe: How long until you need the money? For short-term goals (like buying a car in 2 years), you might choose safer investments. For long-term goals (like retirement in 30 years), you might invest more in stocks, which can be riskier but offer higher returns over time.

Amount Needed: Knowing how much money you'll need helps you figure out how much you need to save and invest regularly.

Risk Tolerance: If your goal is far away, you might be more comfortable taking bigger risks for the chance of higher returns. If your goal is close, you might prefer safer investments.

By setting clear investment goals, you create a roadmap for your financial journey. It helps you stay focused, make smart choices, and track your progress. Think of it as your personal investment GPS, guiding you to where you want to be financially. Here are some guidelines for setting clear investment goals:

Do not set unrealistic investment goals.

You should avoid making plans to achieve something too difficult or impossible with your investment. It's like you're saving money but expecting it to double in just a few months. This is usually not realistic. Instead, aim for goals that are possible, like gradually growing your money over several years.

It's like planning to run a marathon without ever having jogged before. It's important to set achievable goals and make sense of your situation.

Be Realistic About Returns: Expecting your investment to grow too fast can lead to disappointment. Mutual funds usually grow your money over time, not overnight. It's like planting a tree; you can't expect it to bear fruit in just a few days.

Understand Market Conditions: Just like weather affects a farmer's crops, market conditions affect your investments. Sometimes the market does well, sometimes not. You can't expect sunshine every day, so plan for some rainy days in your investment journey too.

Know Your Time Frame: If you need your money back in a short time, it's not realistic to expect huge growth. It's like expecting to become a professional chef after just one cooking class. If you have a longer time to invest, your money has more time to grow.

Consider Your Risk Tolerance: If you're not comfortable with risk, don't set goals that require risky investments. It's like if you're scared of heights, you shouldn't set a goal to climb a tall ladder. Stick with what feels comfortable for you.

Be Patient: Good things take time. If you're saving for a long-term goal, like retirement, give your investments time to grow. It's like training for that marathon; you start slow and build up over time.

So, setting unrealistic goals is like planning to fly to the moon with a homemade rocket. It's great to aim high, but your goals should be based on what's possible and sensible for you.

Neglecting to define short-term and long-term objectives.

It means not making clear plans for what you want to achieve soon (like within a few months or years) and what you want to achieve later on (like in several years or decades). It's like going on a trip without deciding if you're going for a weekend getaway or a long vacation. Knowing your short-term and long-term goals helps you make better choices about saving and investing your money.

When you "neglect to define short-term and long-term objectives," you're basically skipping a very important step in planning your financial future. It's like setting out on a road trip without knowing your final destination or the stops you want to make along the way.

Short-Term Objectives:
These are goals you want to achieve soon, usually within the next few years.
For example, saving for a new laptop, a holiday trip, or building an emergency fund.
These goals usually require safer investment choices because you'll need the money sooner and can't risk big market changes.

Long-Term Objectives:
These are your goals for the distant future, often several years or decades away.
Examples include saving for retirement, your child's college education, or buying a dream home.
For these, you might choose investments that grow over time, like stocks or mutual funds. Since you have more time, you can ride out ups and downs in the market.

<u>*Why Defining These is Important:*</u>
Better Financial Planning: Knowing your goals helps you plan how much to save and invest. Like planning a trip, you decide how much fuel (money) you need and when to refuel (invest more).

Appropriate Risk Taking: Short-term goals usually mean less risk, so you don't lose what you've saved right before you need it. Long-term goals can handle more risk since you have time to recover from any market dips.

Motivation and Tracking: Clear goals keep you motivated. It's easier to save when you know what you're saving for. Plus, you can track your progress, like marking milestones on a map.

Avoiding Impulsive Decisions: When you know your goals, you're less likely to make hasty financial decisions. It's like knowing your route so well that you don't get distracted by every interesting detour.

In summary, not setting short-term and long-term objectives is like sailing without a compass; you might keep moving, but you won't necessarily get where you want to go. By defining these objectives, you give yourself a clear financial direction and a better chance of reaching your destinations.

Failing to align goals with investment horizon.

It means not matching your goals within the right time frame. For example, if you're saving for something you need in 2 years, like a car, you shouldn't choose an investment that's meant for long-term goals, like saving for retirement in 30 years.

It's like wearing beach clothes in the snow – not suitable for the situation. You want your investment choice to fit the time you have to reach your goal.

For example, you are planning for different events in your life but not considering how much time you have for each.

Imagine you have two main goals: buying a new bike next year and saving for retirement which is 30 years away. Each goal has its own 'investment horizon' – the time you have until you need the money.

Short-Term Goals (like buying the bike):
Since this goal is close, you should pick investments that are less risky and more liquid (easy to convert to cash). It's like preparing for a rainstorm that's coming soon; you wouldn't plan a picnic, you'd bring an umbrella.

Long-Term Goals (like retirement):
Here, you have more time. You can choose investments that might have ups and downs in the short term but grow more over many years. It's like planting a tree; it takes time to grow, but eventually, it provides shade.

Overlooking the Importance of Goal Reassessment

When it comes to investing in mutual funds, one common mistake is not reassessing your goals regularly. Imagine your life as a long road trip.

When you started, you might have had a specific destination in mind. But as you drive along, you realize there might be more interesting or suitable places to visit.

Similarly, your life changes over time – you might get a new job, have a family, or your financial situation might change. These changes can affect what you want and need from your investments.

Regularly reassessing your investment goals is like periodically checking your map and making sure you're still on the best route. Maybe you initially invested for long-term growth, but now you need some of that money sooner for a down payment on a house. Or perhaps you were saving for your child's education, but now they've earned a scholarship, and you can focus more on your retirement.

Reassessing also helps you adjust to changes in the market. Economic conditions can affect the performance of mutual funds. What looked like a good investment five years ago might not be the best choice today.

Here's what you can do:
Schedule Regular Reviews: Set a reminder to review your goals and investments once a year or whenever there's a major life event.
Stay Informed: Keep up with market trends and economic news. This knowledge can help you make more informed decisions.

Be Flexible: Be willing to adjust your plans. If your goals change, your investment strategy might need to change too.

Consult Professionals: Talk to financial advisors regularly. They can provide valuable insights and help you stay on track.

In summary, not reassessing your goals is like sticking to an outdated map. To reach your destination successfully, you need to periodically check your route and make adjustments as needed.

Ignoring the Impact of Life Changes on Investment Goals

Life is full of changes – some planned, some unexpected. These changes can significantly impact your investment goals. For example, getting married, having a child, changing jobs, or facing a health issue can alter your financial priorities and capabilities. Ignoring these life changes while investing in mutual funds is like trying to fit into an old outfit that no longer suits your current style or size – it's uncomfortable and impractical.

When major life events occur, they can shift what you need and want from your investments. For instance, if you start a family, you might want to focus more on securing your child's future, leading you to consider more conservative investment options. On the other hand, a career advancement with a higher salary might allow you to take on more risk or save more for retirement.

Here's how to handle this:
Reevaluate Regularly: Whenever you experience a significant life change, take time to reassess your financial goals.

Adjust Investments Accordingly: Depending on the change, you may need to increase your savings rate, switch to less risky investment options, or realign your portfolio to match your new goals.

Emergency Fund: Always maintain an emergency fund. Life's unpredictability makes it crucial to have readily accessible funds without disrupting your investment strategy.

Seek Professional Advice: A financial advisor can help you navigate through these changes and suggest adjustments to your investment plan.

Failing to consider life changes in your investment strategy is like following an outdated map. As your life evolves, so should your investment approach, ensuring it remains aligned with your current and future needs.

Not Considering Risk Tolerance in Goal Setting

When setting investment goals, many individuals overlook a crucial factor i.e., their own risk tolerance. Risk tolerance is essentially how comfortable you are with the ups and downs in the value of your investments. It's like riding a roller coaster; some people enjoy the thrill of the highest peaks and steepest drops, while others prefer a gentler ride.

If you're not comfortable with high-risk investments, setting a goal that requires investing heavily in volatile stocks can lead to anxiety and poor decision-making. On the flip side, if you have a high-risk tolerance, being too conservative might lead to frustration or missed opportunities for higher returns.

Understanding your risk tolerance involves:
Self-Assessment: Be honest with yourself about how much risk you can handle. Think about how you would feel if your investments dropped in value temporarily.

Consider Your Time Horizon: Generally, the longer your investment period, the more risk you can afford to take. If your goal is many years away, you have more time to recover from market dips.

Life Situation: Your age, income stability, and financial responsibilities play a role in determining your risk tolerance.

Review and Adjust: Your risk tolerance can change over time, so it's important to reassess it periodically.

Neglecting to consider risk tolerance in goal setting is like ignoring the weather forecast before a hike. By aligning your investment goals with your risk tolerance, you ensure a more comfortable and suitable investment journey.

Setting Goals Without Considering Liquidity Needs

When setting investment goals, it's crucial to consider your liquidity needs. Liquidity refers to how quickly and easily you can convert your investments into cash without significant loss. It's like having enough water in your backpack during a hike – you need to be sure you can access it when you need it.

If you overlook liquidity, you might find yourself in a situation where you need cash, but your money is tied up in investments that you can't sell easily or without losing value. This is especially important for short-term goals or emergencies.

To balance this:
Emergency Fund: Always have an easily accessible emergency fund that's not tied up in investments.

Understand Investment Liquidity: Different investments have different levels of liquidity. Stocks are generally more liquid than real estate, for instance.

Match Investments with Cash Needs: If you anticipate needing cash in the near future, choose investments that can be easily and quickly liquidated.

Regularly Review Cash Flow: Keep an eye on your incoming and outgoing funds. This will help you understand your liquidity needs and adjust your investments accordingly.

Neglecting to consider liquidity needs is like going on a desert trek without a water bottle. By ensuring you have sufficient liquidity, you maintain the flexibility to meet financial needs as they arise without disrupting your long-term investment strategy.

Failing to communicate goals to financial advisors effectively.

Failing to effectively communicate your goals to your financial advisor is like going on a journey without telling the driver where you want to go. Your financial advisor needs to know what you're saving for, when you need the money, and how much risk you're comfortable with.

For example, if you're saving for retirement, your child's college fund, and a new house, each goal might need a different investment approach. If your financial advisor doesn't know all your goals, they might not pick the best mutual funds for you.

Also, if something in your life changes, like getting a new job or having a baby, you should tell your advisor. These changes can affect your investment plans.

Lastly, it's important to discuss how much risk you're willing to take. Some people are okay with a bit of risk for potentially higher returns, while others prefer safer investments.

In short, good communication with your financial advisor ensures that they can guide you properly and choose mutual funds that match your needs and goals.

SELF-ASSESSMENT

Investment Goals Clarity Questionnaire

I hope you have read the previous chapter carefully and I am sure some questions might be arising in your mind by now.

To find answers to those questions that are coming to your mind, and to decide whether you have defined your investment goals clearly, you will find below a detailed questionnaire that will help you in making your decision.

The scoring points for these questionnaires are specified below:

Never	=	4
Rarely	=	3
Sometimes	=	2
Often	=	1
Always	=	0

QUESTION SET

1. How often do you invest without a specific financial goal in mind?

Answer: [   ]

2. Do you regularly review and update your financial goals?

Answer: [   ]

3. Are you clear about when you will need to use the money you are investing?

Answer: [   ]

4. Do you set investment goals based on your personal financial needs rather than market trends?

Answer: [   ]

5. How frequently do you revisit your risk tolerance to ensure it aligns with your current life situation?

Answer: [   ]

6. Do you consider the impact of inflation on your long-term investment goals?

Answer: [   ]

7. How often do you adjust your investment strategy to stay aligned with your financial goals?

Answer: [   ]

8. Do you set specific and measurable financial goals for your investments?

Answer: [   ]

9. How often do you base your investment decisions on advice from friends, family, or social media, without considering your personal financial goals?

Answer: [   ]

10. Are you confident in explaining your investment goals to a financial advisor or planner?

Answer: [   ]

SCORING

Total up your points. A lower score indicates clearer and well-defined investment goals, while a higher score suggests a need for more clarity in goal setting and strategy.

0-10 Points: Excellent clarity in investment goals.

11-20 Points: Good understanding, but some aspects need refinement.

21-30 Points: Moderate clarity, consider revisiting your goals and strategy.

31-40 Points: Your investment goals are not well-defined, seek advice to improve.

NOTES:

_____

_____

_____

_____

_____

_____

_____

_____

_____

2.
RISK TOLERANCE AND ASSET ALLOCATION

Risk Tolerance: We already discussed in the previous chapter about roller coaster rides. It's like how much of a roller coaster ride you can handle. Some people love big, scary roller coasters with lots of ups and downs.

Others prefer a gentler ride that doesn't make their stomach turn. In investing, risk tolerance is about how many ups and downs in your investment value you can handle without worrying. If you're okay seeing the value of your investments go up and down a lot, you have a high-risk tolerance. If not, you have a low-risk tolerance.

Asset Allocation: This is like planning a balanced diet. You don't eat just one type of food; you have a mix – some fruits, vegetables, grains, proteins, etc.

In investing, asset allocation means spreading your investments across different types of assets – like stocks, bonds, and cash. Stocks are like spicy food – they can offer big flavors (returns) but can be hard to stomach for some. Bonds are more like bread – usually steadier and less dramatic. Cash is like water – it doesn't grow, but it's safe and necessary.

By understanding your risk tolerance, you decide how much of each type of investment (asset) you should have. If you can handle the roller coaster, you might have more stocks. If not, you might stick with more bonds and cash. This helps you build a portfolio that suits your comfort level and goals.

Underestimating Personal Risk Tolerance

When choosing mutual funds, a common mistake is underestimating how much investment risk you can comfortably handle. It's like thinking you can easily lift heavy weights without prior training. If the market gets rough and your investments lose value, you might panic and sell at a loss, harming your long-term financial health.

Your risk tolerance is how much market ups and downs you can endure without worrying too much. It depends on factors like your age, income stability, savings, and how you react to stressful financial situations. Younger investors with stable jobs and long-term perspectives might tolerate more risk, aiming for higher returns. Conversely, those nearing retirement or with unstable incomes might prefer less risk.

It's crucial to honestly assess your risk comfort level before investing. Overestimating your tolerance can lead to anxiety and poor decisions in volatile markets. A balanced approach, where you're not constantly worried about your investments, is key to successful long-term investing. Remember, understanding your true risk tolerance helps in selecting mutual funds that align with your comfort level, ensuring a smoother investment journey.

Relying Solely on Financial Advisor Risk Assessments

Depending solely on a financial advisor's assessment of risk can be a misstep in mutual fund investing. It's like always following a GPS without checking the road signs yourself. Advisors provide valuable guidance, but their risk evaluation may not fully capture your personal feelings about money and risk.

Financial advisors typically use standardized questionnaires to gauge risk tolerance, focusing on age, income, investment goals, and financial situation. However, these assessments might not consider your unique life experiences, emotional reactions to market changes, or personal financial fears.

You know your financial situation and emotional reactions better than anyone else. It's important to actively participate in the risk assessment process and communicate your concerns and expectations clearly to your advisor. This collaboration ensures a more accurate reflection of your risk tolerance, leading to better investment choices.

In essence, while advisors play a crucial role in the investment process, remember it's your money at stake. Stay engaged, ask questions, and ensure the final investment strategy resonates with your personal comfort level regarding risk.

Neglecting to Reassess Risk Tolerance Periodically

Not regularly reassessing your risk tolerance when investing in mutual funds is like never updating your wardrobe as you age. Just as your clothing preferences change over time, so can your comfort with investment risk.

Various life events can alter your risk tolerance. These include major changes like getting married, having children, changing jobs, or nearing retirement. Each of these life stages might influence how much financial risk you're willing to take. For instance, as retirement approaches, you might prefer more stable, lower-risk investments.

It's crucial to periodically review your investment strategy and ensure it still fits your current life situation. This might mean rebalancing your portfolio to reflect a change in risk tolerance. Failing to do this can lead to a mismatch between your investments and your actual risk comfort level.

Regularly updating your risk assessment helps in maintaining an investment portfolio that reflects your current needs and goals. It's a vital step in ensuring your investments are always aligned with your changing life circumstances and financial objectives.

Misunderstanding the Concept of Asset Allocation

Misunderstanding asset allocation in mutual fund investing is like misusing a map; you might have the right tool, but if you don't know how to read it, you won't get to your destination. Asset allocation is the process of distributing your investments among different asset classes, such as stocks, bonds, and cash.

The goal of asset allocation is to balance risk and reward according to your investment goals, risk tolerance, and investment horizon. Each asset class has different levels of risk and return, so how you allocate your assets can significantly impact your investment outcome.

For example, stocks are generally riskier but offer higher potential returns, while bonds are typically more stable but provide lower returns. The right mix for you will depend on how much risk you can tolerate and how long you plan to invest.

Misunderstanding asset allocation can lead to an imbalanced portfolio, either too risky or too conservative for your needs. For instance, a heavily stock-weighted portfolio might be too volatile if you're nearing retirement. On the other hand, overly conservative investments might not provide the growth needed to reach long-term goals like retirement savings.

Proper asset allocation is dynamic; it should evolve as your life circumstances and financial goals change. It's essential to understand and regularly review your asset allocation to ensure it aligns with your current objectives and risk tolerance.

Overemphasizing or Neglecting Certain Asset Classes

Overemphasizing or neglecting certain asset classes in mutual fund investing is like packing for a vacation and only bringing beachwear, even though you're going to the mountains too. Just as you need different clothes for different environments, you need a variety of investments for a balanced portfolio.

Overemphasizing one asset class, like putting most of your money in stocks, can lead to high volatility and risk. If the stock market drops, your portfolio could suffer significantly. On the other hand, neglecting certain asset classes, like avoiding stocks entirely for fear of risk, might limit your portfolio's growth potential.

A well-balanced portfolio includes a mix of different asset classes, each contributing to your overall investment goals in different ways. Stocks offer growth potential, bonds provide stability and income, and other assets like real estate or commodities can offer diversification benefits.

The key is to find the right balance that suits your investment goals and risk tolerance. This balance should be reviewed and adjusted over time, especially as your financial situation and market conditions change. Overemphasizing or neglecting certain asset classes can lead to an unbalanced portfolio, not aligned with your investment objectives and risk profile.

Reacting Emotionally to Short-Term Market Fluctuations

Reacting emotionally to short-term market fluctuations when investing in mutual funds is like changing your entire travel plan just because of a little rain. Markets naturally go up and down, but making investment decisions based on these short-term movements can harm your long-term financial goals.

Emotional reactions, like panic selling when the market drops or greedily investing during a market high, can lead to poor investment choices. These reactions are often driven by fear or excitement, rather than a rational assessment of your investment strategy.

It's important to remember that market fluctuations are normal and to be expected. A well-thought-out investment strategy considers these ups and downs and focuses on long-term goals. Reacting to short-term market changes can derail this strategy, potentially leading to missed opportunities and reduced returns.

Staying calm and sticking to your investment plan during market volatility is crucial. It helps to remember your long-term objectives and trust the investment process. Consulting with a financial advisor during turbulent times can also provide perspective and guidance, helping you make decisions based on logic rather than emotion.

In summary, avoiding emotional reactions to market fluctuations is key to maintaining a steady course toward your investment goals. Keeping a long-term perspective and adhering to your planned strategy can lead to better investment outcomes.

Forgetting the Impact of Inflation on Risk Tolerance

Overlooking inflation when considering your risk tolerance in mutual fund investments is like forgetting about the rising cost of living while planning your budget. Inflation reduces the purchasing power of money over time, meaning what $100 buys today might cost more in the future. If your investments don't grow at a rate that outpaces inflation, you're effectively losing money in terms of what it can buy.

For example, if inflation is at 3% per year and your investment only grows by 2%, you're not keeping up with the increasing cost of goods and services. This is especially crucial for long-term goals like retirement. If your investment strategy is too conservative, you might not accumulate enough to maintain your desired lifestyle in the future.

Therefore, when assessing risk tolerance, consider if your investments can grow enough to beat inflation. This often means accepting a certain level of risk to achieve higher returns. It's a balancing act between protecting your money and growing it sufficiently to ensure its future purchasing power.

Ignoring the Role of Time Horizon in Risk Assessment

Ignoring the time horizon in risk assessment for mutual funds is like planning a trip without considering the travel time. Your investment time horizon is the period you plan to keep your money invested before you need it. This is crucial in determining how much risk you can take.

For short-term goals (like saving for a car in 2 years), a lower-risk strategy is typically better because you need the money soon and can't afford big market dips. For long-term goals (like retirement in 30 years), you have more time to recover from market fluctuations, allowing for a higher-risk strategy that potentially offers greater returns.

Not aligning your investments with your time horizon can lead to two main issues: taking too much risk for short-term goals, risking significant losses right when you need the money, or being too conservative for long-term goals, missing out on higher growth opportunities. Understanding your time horizon ensures that your investment strategy is tailored to when you need the funds, balancing risk and return in a way that suits your timeline.

SELF-ASSESSMENT

Risk Tolerance and Asset Allocation Questionnaire

I hope you have read the previous chapter carefully and I am sure some questions might be arising in your mind by now.

To find answers to those questions that are coming to your mind, and to decide whether you have defined your investment goals clearly, you will find below a detailed questionnaire that will help you in making your decision.

The scoring points for these questionnaires are specified below:

Never	=	4
Rarely	=	3
Sometimes	=	2
Often	=	1
Always	=	0

QUESTION SET

1. How often do you review your investments to check if they align with your risk tolerance?

Answer: [   ]

2. Do you understand the level of risk associated with each asset class (stocks, bonds, etc.) in your portfolio?

Answer: [   ]

3. How frequently do you adjust your investments based on changes in your life circumstances (like age, income change, etc.)?

Answer: [   ]

4. Do you regularly assess how comfortable you are with the possibility of losing money on your investments?

Answer: [   ]

5. How often do you diversify your investments across different asset classes to spread risk?

Answer: [   ]

6. Are you proactive in rebalancing your portfolio to maintain your desired asset allocation?

Answer: [   ]

7. How frequently do you evaluate your investments to ensure they align with your long-term financial goals?

Answer: [   ]

8. Do you consider how market fluctuations could impact your investment strategy and risk level?

Answer: [   ]

9. Are you aware of how your emotional reactions to market changes can affect your investment decisions?

Answer: [   ]

10. How often do you consult with a financial advisor to assess and adjust your risk tolerance and asset allocation?

Answer: [   ]

SCORING:

Total up your points. A lower score indicates a strong alignment of your investments with your risk tolerance and well-thought-out asset allocation. In comparison, a higher score suggests areas for improvement in understanding and managing your investment risk and strategy.

0-10 Points: Excellent alignment with risk tolerance and asset allocation.

11-20 Points: Good awareness, but some fine-tuning may be beneficial.

21-30 Points: Moderate understanding; reassessment of investment approach recommended.

31-40 Points: Your investment strategy may not align well with your risk tolerance; consider seeking professional advice for better alignment.

NOTES:

_____

_____

_____

_____

_____

_____

3.
NAVIGATING INVESTMENT STYLES

Navigating investment styles in mutual funds is about choosing a strategy that matches your financial goals and risk comfort. Think of it as picking the right tool for a job. The main styles are:

Growth Investing: This is like betting on fast-growing companies. The stocks might be pricey, but they have high growth potential. It's a bit riskier, especially in unstable markets.

Value Investing: Here, you look for undervalued or 'bargain' stocks that might increase in value. It's like finding hidden treasures. This style requires patience and a keen eye for potential.

Blend or Balanced Investing: This mixes growth and value investing. It's like having a varied diet to stay healthy. It aims for a balance between steady growth and finding undervalued stocks, reducing risk through diversity.

The key is to pick a style that aligns with how much risk you can handle and what you aim to achieve with your investments.

Not Understanding the Differences Between Growth, Value, and Blend Funds

Understanding mutual funds is akin to understanding different genres in a library. Each genre caters to specific tastes and expectations. Similarly, growth, value, and blend funds each have unique characteristics and cater to different investor profiles.

Growth funds are like science fiction novels - they're about companies expected to grow faster than the market average. These companies often reinvest profits rather than paying dividends, focusing on innovation and expansion. However, they can be riskier, like the unpredictable nature of a sci-fi plot.

Value funds, on the other hand, are more like historical novels. They focus on companies that are currently undervalued in the market but have the potential for appreciation. These companies are often established with steady performance records and may pay dividends. The idea here is akin to finding a classic book undervalued in a second-hand store - it has inherent worth not currently reflected in its price.

Blend funds are like an anthology of short stories, combining elements of both growth and value investing. They offer a balanced approach, suitable for those who prefer a mix of stability and potential growth.

Not understanding these differences can lead you to choose a fund that doesn't align with your expectations or risk tolerance. It's like picking up a book in a genre you don't enjoy - the investment journey might not be as fulfilling or effective as it could be.

Investing in Funds That Don't Match Personal Investment Style

Investing in a mutual fund that doesn't match your investment style is like buying a pair of shoes that don't fit. They might look great and work well for others, but they won't be comfortable for you.

Your investment style reflects your risk tolerance, investment goals, and the time frame for those goals. Some investors have an aggressive style - they're comfortable with higher risks for the potential of higher returns. This is akin to wearing high-heeled shoes for fashion despite discomfort, valuing appearance (or high returns) over comfort.

Others have a more conservative style, prioritizing the preservation of capital over high returns. This is like choosing comfortable sneakers over stylish but uncomfortable shoes.

Some prefer a balanced style - a mix of aggressive and conservative investments, like owning a variety of shoes for different occasions.

Investing in a fund that doesn't match your style can lead to discomfort, worry, and potential financial strain. It's essential to understand and be honest about your style to make investment choices that you're comfortable with and that align with your financial goals.

Neglecting to Diversify Investment Styles Within a Portfolio

A well-diversified investment portfolio is like a well-balanced diet. Just as you need a variety of foods for good health, you need a mix of investment styles for a healthy portfolio. Neglecting to diversify across different investment styles can expose you to unnecessary risks and volatility.

Just as relying solely on carbohydrates or proteins isn't healthy, relying solely on one investment style (like only growth or only value) can lead to imbalanced financial health. Diversification across styles allows you to balance the risks and rewards. For instance, when growth stocks are performing well, value stocks might be underperforming, and vice versa.

Additionally, different investment styles react differently to market conditions. Certain foods are better in specific seasons, certain investment styles may perform better in specific economic environments.

Without diversification, your portfolio might be overly exposed to the risks of a single style. It's like eating only your favorite food - it might be enjoyable, but it's not healthy in the long run. A well-diversified portfolio, on the other hand, can weather different market conditions more effectively.

Overemphasizing a Single Investment Style

Overemphasizing a single investment style in your portfolio is like listening only to one genre of music. While it may be your favorite, it limits your experience and exposure to other enriching genres.

For instance, if you focus solely on growth funds, you might miss out on the potential stability and undervalued opportunities that value funds offer. Similarly, focusing only on value funds might mean missing out on the high growth potential of some companies.

This overemphasis can lead to a lack of balance in your portfolio, making it more susceptible to market fluctuations associated with that particular style. During times when your chosen style underperforms, your entire portfolio could suffer significantly.

Diversifying across different investment styles ensures a more balanced approach, allowing for potential gains across different market conditions and reducing the risk of significant losses tied to one specific style. It's about creating a symphony with different types of music, each complementing the other.

Failing to Adapt Investment Styles to Changing Market Conditions

Failing to adapt investment styles to changing market conditions is akin to wearing winter clothes in summer. Just as clothing choices change with the seasons, investment choices should change with market conditions.

Market conditions can vary greatly over time – periods of rapid growth, market corrections, or economic recessions. Sticking rigidly to one investment style, regardless of these changes, can lead to missed opportunities or increased risk.

For example, during a market upswing, growth funds may offer substantial returns. However, in a declining market, value or more conservative funds might provide better stability. Adapting your investment strategy to these conditions can help maximize returns and minimize losses.

This adaptability requires staying informed about market trends and economic forecasts and being willing to make changes to your investment approach. It's about being flexible and responsive, ensuring that your investment strategy remains effective and relevant in varying market climates.

Not Considering Sector-Specific Risks in Investment Styles

When investing in mutual funds, it's crucial to understand that different sectors of the economy carry different risks. Not considering these sector-specific risks is like a chef not considering the unique flavors and cooking times of different ingredients. Each sector – be it technology, healthcare, energy, or finance – has its own set of dynamics and risk factors.

For example, the technology sector is known for its high growth potential, but it can also be highly volatile, and sensitive to changes in consumer trends, and regulatory environments. On the other hand, sectors like utilities or consumer staples might not offer the same growth potential but tend to be more stable during economic downturns.

Ignoring these differences can lead to an imbalanced portfolio. It's akin to putting all your eggs in one basket or, in cooking terms, using only one type of spice for every dish. This lack of diversification can increase your investment risk if the sector you're heavily invested in faces a downturn.

A savvy investor recognizes these sector-specific risks and balances them accordingly. This involves diversifying your investments across various sectors, much like a chef balances the flavors in a meal. This way, if one sector experiences a downturn, your entire portfolio isn't significantly impacted. Understanding and managing these risks is key to a well-rounded and resilient investment approach.

Chasing Trends Without Understanding Their Sustainability

Chasing investment trends without understanding their sustainability is like following a crowd without knowing where they're going. In the investment world, trends can come and go rapidly. A sector or style that is the current 'hot pick' might not be a wise choice in the long term.

Investors often get caught up in the excitement of a trending sector or style, pouring money into it without considering whether the trend is based on solid fundamentals. It's essential to distinguish between a genuine, sustainable trend and a short-term fad.

Sustainable trends are backed by strong fundamentals like technological innovations, demographic shifts, or changes in consumer behavior. In contrast, fads might be based on speculation or short-term events with no long-lasting impact.

Investing based on trend-chasing can lead to significant losses when the trend reverses. It's like buying a ticket for a hype train that soon runs out of steam. A more prudent approach involves researching and understanding the reasons behind a trend and evaluating its long-term viability before investing.

Investing in Funds with Conflicting Investment Styles

Investing in funds with conflicting investment styles is like trying to mix oil and water – they don't blend well. Each investment style has its philosophy, risk profile, and set of expectations. When combined without a clear strategy, they can work against each other, reducing the effectiveness of your portfolio.

For example, if you invest in both a fund that aggressively pursues high-growth tech stocks and another that focuses on conservative, dividend-paying stocks, the conflicting strategies can negate each other's benefits. In certain market conditions, one will perform well while the other suffers, leading to an overall imbalance in your portfolio performance.

The key is to have a coherent investment strategy where each fund complements rather than conflicts with the others. This doesn't mean all your funds must have the same style, but rather that they should be chosen with an understanding of how they fit together in the context of your overall portfolio.

A well-structured portfolio considers how each fund contributes to your investment objectives, risk tolerance, and time horizon. It's like building a team where each member brings different skills and strengths that, when combined, work towards a common goal effectively. Selecting funds with complementary styles is crucial for creating a well-balanced and efficient portfolio.

SELF-ASSESSMENT

Investment Style Assessment Questionnaire

I hope you have read the previous chapter carefully and I am sure some questions might be arising in your mind by now.

To find answers to those questions that are coming to your mind, and to decide whether you have analyzed your investment style clearly, you will find below a detailed questionnaire that will help you in making your decision.

The scoring points for these questionnaires are specified below:

Never	=	4
Rarely	=	3
Sometimes	=	2
Often	=	1
Always	=	0

QUESTION SET

1. Do you invest in funds without understanding their investment strategy (growth, value, index, etc.)?

Answer: [   ]

2. How often do you review the historical performance of a fund before investing?

Answer: [   ]

3. Do you consider how a fund fits with your risk tolerance when making investment decisions?

Answer: [   ]

4. How frequently do you adjust your portfolio based on changes in your financial goals?

Answer: [   ]

5. Do you regularly assess whether your investments align with your long-term financial objectives?

Answer: [   ]

6. How often do you invest based on market trends without considering if they match your investment philosophy?

Answer: [   ]

7. Do you diversify your investments across different asset classes (stocks, bonds, etc.)?

Answer: [   ]

8. How frequently do you review and rebalance your portfolio to maintain your desired asset allocation?

Answer: [   ]

9. Do you consider the tax implications of your investment choices?

Answer: [   ]

10. How often do you consult with a financial advisor to ensure your investments are in line with your investment style?

Answer: [   ]

SCORING:

Total up your points. A lower score indicates that your investment choices are well-aligned with your investment style, while a higher score suggests a need for a better understanding and alignment of your investment approach with your personal preferences and goals.

0-10 Points: Excellent alignment with personal investment style.

11-20 Points: Good, but some aspects of your investment style might need more attention.

21-30 Points: Moderate alignment; reassessment and adjustment of investment style recommended.

31-40 Points: Your investment choices may not be well-aligned with your style; consider seeking professional advice for better alignment.

NOTES:

_____

_____

_____

_____

_____

_____

_____

4.
FEES AND EXPENSES DEMYSTIFIED

"Fees and Expenses Demystified" in the context of mutual funds is about understanding the various costs associated with your investment. Like buying a car where you consider both the purchase price and the maintenance costs, in mutual funds, it's not just about the returns but also the fees and expenses that come with them.

Expense Ratio: This is an annual fee, expressed as a percentage of your investment, that covers the fund's operational costs, including management, administration, and marketing. A higher expense ratio can eat into your returns over time.

Sales Load: Some funds charge a sales load, which is a fee for buying or selling shares. A front-end load is paid when you buy shares, while a back-end load (also called a deferred sales charge) is paid when you sell shares.

Other Fees: These might include transaction fees for buying/selling within the fund, and sometimes performance fees if the fund exceeds certain benchmarks.

Understanding these fees is crucial because they can significantly impact your net returns. The key is to find a balance between reasonable fees and the quality or potential of the fund. Always read the fund prospectus to clearly understand all associated fees before investing.

Ignoring the Impact of Fees on Overall Returns

Overlooking the impact of fees on mutual fund investments is like ignoring small leaks in a bucket of water. Over time, these leaks can significantly reduce the amount of water in the bucket.

Similarly, fees, even if they seem small, can considerably diminish your investment returns over time. Each fee taken from your fund is a portion of your potential earnings being removed.

For instance, if a fund has high management fees or other charges, a substantial portion of your returns could be consumed by these fees, especially in the long run.

It's crucial to understand that the money paid in fees doesn't contribute to your investment growth. As such, lower fees can lead to more money staying invested and compounding over time, potentially leading to better net returns.

It's important to pay attention to all fees associated with a mutual fund and understand how they impact your investment in the long run.

Not Understanding the Various Types of Fees Associated with Mutual Funds

Not being aware of the different types of fees in mutual funds is like navigating a city without understanding its transportation costs.

Various fees can be charged in mutual funds, each affecting your investment differently. These include management fees (for running the fund), administrative fees (for fund operations), and distribution fees (also known as 12b-1 fees, for marketing and distribution costs).

Additionally, funds may charge transaction fees for buying or selling securities, or redemption fees if you sell your shares within a certain period.

Some funds also have sales charges (loads) either when you buy (front-end loads) or sell (back-end loads) shares.

Understanding these fees is essential as they can significantly impact the fund's overall returns. Knowing what each fee entails and how it affects your investment can help you make more cost-effective investment decisions.

Falling for Hidden Fees and Charges

Falling for hidden fees in mutual funds is like incurring unexpected charges on a hotel bill. These are the costs that aren't immediately apparent when you first invest in a fund.

Hidden fees can include costs for excessive trading within the fund, performance fees, or account service fees for smaller account balances. Sometimes, these fees are buried in the fund's prospectus and not prominently disclosed.

Investors need to diligently review the fund's prospectus and annual reports or consult with a financial advisor to understand all the potential fees and how they can impact the investment.

Being vigilant about hidden fees can help you avoid paying more than necessary and ensure that more of your money is working for you.

Assuming Higher Fees Guarantee Better Performance

Believing that higher fees guarantee better performance in mutual funds is like thinking that the most expensive restaurant always has the best food.

In reality, higher fees don't necessarily mean better returns. These fees are often associated with actively managed funds, where fund managers make decisions about buying and selling stocks.

However, numerous studies have shown that not all actively managed funds consistently outperform the market or their lower-fee counterparts, especially after accounting for their fees.

It's essential to compare the historical performance of funds relative to their fees. A fund with lower fees that performs comparably or better than a higher-fee fund can be a more cost-effective choice.

Investors should critically analyze whether the potential for higher returns justifies the higher fees and not assume that paying more always means getting more.

Overlooking the Impact of Fees on Long-Term Returns

Ignoring the impact of fees on long-term returns is like disregarding small water leaks in a boat; over time, they can significantly affect its buoyancy.

Fees may seem small on an annual basis, but their impact over time can be substantial. Even a 1% higher fee can mean a significant amount of money lost to fees over an investment horizon of 20 or 30 years.

This is because not only do you lose the amount paid in fees, but you also lose the growth that this money could have generated if it had remained invested. When evaluating mutual funds, consider the cumulative effect of fees over the entire period you plan to hold the fund.

Compare the long-term performance of funds net of fees to understand the true impact on your returns. Lower fee funds can sometimes leave you with more money in your pocket, even if their performance is slightly lower than higher fee funds.

Failing to Consider the Impact of Taxes on Net Returns

Not considering the impact of taxes on net returns from mutual funds is like forgetting to account for tax deductions in your salary.

Mutual fund distributions, whether from dividends or capital gains, are often subject to taxes, which can reduce your actual returns.

The tax impact varies depending on the type of fund, the holding period, and your tax bracket. For instance, funds that frequently buy and sell securities can generate higher capital gains distributions, leading to a larger tax bill for the investor.

It's important to consider the tax efficiency of a fund, especially if you are investing in a taxable account. Some funds are designed to be tax-efficient, making them more suitable for such accounts.

Understanding the tax implications can help you better estimate the actual returns you will receive and make more informed investment choices.

Ignoring the Compounding Effect of Fees Over Time

Overlooking the compounding effect of fees over time is like ignoring interest accumulation on a debt. Just as compound interest can significantly increase debt over time, compounded fees can substantially reduce your investment growth.

Each dollar paid in fees is a dollar not earned returns. Over years or decades, the amount lost to fees can grow exponentially due to the foregone opportunity of these fees compounding along with the rest of your investment.

For example, a 2% fee might not seem like much in one year, but over 30 years, it can consume a significant portion of your potential earnings. This compounding effect is why it's crucial to consider not just the returns that a fund generates, but also the net returns after all fees.

Lower fee funds can sometimes result in higher net wealth accumulation over the long term, even if their gross returns are not the highest.

Not Evaluating the Value Provided by Actively Managed Funds

Not evaluating the value provided by actively managed funds is like buying a premium service without assessing its benefits.

Actively managed funds are managed by professional fund managers who actively make investment decisions, aiming to outperform the market. These funds typically have higher fees than passively managed funds, like index funds, which simply track a market index.

However, the additional cost of actively managed funds can be justified if they provide significant value, such as superior performance, risk management, or access to specific markets or sectors that are not easily accessible through passive funds.

It's important to evaluate whether the potential benefits of active management outweigh the higher fees. This involves looking at the fund's track record, the expertise of the fund manager, the fund's investment strategy, and its performance relative to its benchmark and peers after accounting for fees.

In some market conditions or investment sectors, the active management approach might offer advantages that justify the higher cost. However, this is not universally true and should be assessed on a case-by-case basis.

SELF-ASSESSMENT

Mutual Fund Fees and Expenses
Understanding Questionnaire

I hope you have read the previous chapter carefully and I am sure some questions might be arising in your mind by now.

To find answers to those questions that are coming to your mind, and to decide whether you understand mutual fund fees and related expenses, you will find below a detailed questionnaire that will help you in making your decision.

The scoring points for these questionnaires are specified below:

Never	=	4
Rarely	=	3
Sometimes	=	2
Often	=	1
Always	=	0

QUESTION SET

1. Do you check the expense ratio of a mutual fund before investing?

Answer: [   ]

2. Are you aware of any transaction fees associated with buying or selling a fund?

Answer: [   ]

3. Do you consider the impact of management fees on your potential returns?

Answer: [   ]

4. How often do you compare fees when choosing between similar mutual funds?

Answer: [   ]

5. Are you aware of any performance fees charged by your mutual funds?

Answer: [   ]

6. Do you investigate any 12b-1 fees (marketing or distribution fees) that a fund may charge?

Answer: [   ]

7. How often do you review the total cost of ownership of your mutual fund investments?

Answer: [   ]

8. Do you consider the tax implications of the mutual fund's turnover rate?

Answer: [   ]

9. Are you familiar with any redemption fees your mutual funds may charge?

Answer: [   ]

10. Do you regularly monitor for any changes in the fee structure of your mutual funds?

Answer: [   ]

SCORING:

Total up your points. The lower the score, the better your understanding of mutual fund fees and expenses. High scores indicate areas where you may need to increase your knowledge to make more informed investment decisions.

0-10 Points: Excellent understanding of mutual fund fees and expenses.

11-20 Points: Good awareness, but there may be some gaps in understanding.

21-30 Points: Moderate understanding; further education on mutual fund fees recommended.

31-40 Points: Limited understanding of fees; significant learning required to effectively manage mutual fund investments.

NOTES:

_____

_____

_____

_____

_____

_____

_____

PART II:
COMMON PITFALLS
TO AVOID

5.
CHASING PAST PERFORMANCE

"Chasing past performance" in mutual fund investing means picking funds based only on their historical success.

It's like buying a sports team's jersey just because they won last season. This approach can be misleading because a fund's past success doesn't guarantee future results.

Markets change, and what worked before might not work again. Also, focusing only on past performance ignores other important aspects like fees, the manager's skills, and whether the fund's strategy fits your financial goals.

A better approach is to look at a fund's history as just one piece of the puzzle, considering all factors before investing.

Relying Solely on Historical Returns for Fund Selection

Choosing a mutual fund based only on its historical returns is like driving by only looking in the rearview mirror.

Past performance can offer some insights, but it's not a guarantee of future results. Markets change, and what worked well in the past might not work in the future.

A fund that performed exceptionally well over the last few years might not continue to do so. Investors should also consider other factors such as the fund's investment strategy, risk profile, and how it fits within their overall portfolio.

It's crucial to analyze the fund in the current market context and align it with your investment goals and risk tolerance.

Chasing Recent Top Performers Without Understanding Underlying Factors

Investing in funds just because they've recently performed well is like buying a car simply because it won the last race.

This approach ignores the reasons behind the performance and whether those factors are sustainable.

Recent top performers might have benefited from specific market conditions that may not last. Without understanding the drivers behind a fund's success, you risk investing based on a trend that might reverse.

It's essential to look beneath the surface, examining the fund's investment approach, the sectors it's invested in, and how it aligns with current market trends and your investment strategy.

Ignoring Market Conditions During the Periods of Past Performance

Overlooking the market conditions that contributed to a mutual fund's past performance is like ignoring the weather conditions during a record-breaking athletic performance.

Just as a tailwind can help a runner, certain market conditions can inflate a fund's performance.

For example, a bull market can boost the performance of equity funds, but this may not continue in a bear market.

Understanding the market context during the performance period helps in assessing how the fund might perform under different conditions.

It's important to consider whether the fund's strategy is adaptable to changing market scenarios.

Failing to Consider the Sustainability of Past Performance

Not considering the sustainability of a mutual fund's past performance is like expecting a one-hit wonder to have a series of hit songs.

Past success doesn't always repeat, especially in the dynamic world of investments. Factors like changing market dynamics, economic shifts, and sector rotations can affect a fund's future performance.

It's crucial to evaluate if the fund's past success is due to a consistent, repeatable strategy or if it was a result of temporary market conditions.

Understanding the reasons behind the performance helps in determining if it's likely to be sustainable.

Not Accounting for Changes in Fund Management During the Performance Period

Ignoring changes in a mutual fund's management is like not considering a new coach's impact on a sports team.

Just as a coach can significantly influence a team's performance, a fund manager plays a critical role in a fund's success. Management changes can lead to changes in investment strategy, risk approach, and ultimately, performance.

If a fund has performed well under one manager, there's no guarantee that this will continue with a new manager.

Evaluating the track record and experience of the current management team is essential in assessing a fund's potential future performance.

Disregarding the Importance of Consistent Performance Over Time

Overlooking a fund's consistent performance over time is like ignoring a runner's training record in favor of a few fast races.

Consistency in mutual fund performance is a sign of a fund manager's skill in different market conditions and strategies that can withstand market volatility.

A fund that shows steadiness and reliability over a longer period is often a safer choice than one that has sporadic peaks and troughs.

This consistent performance indicates a fund's ability to navigate various market challenges and sustain growth over time.

Assuming a Fund Will Continue Its Exceptional Performance Indefinitely

Believing that a mutual fund will continue its exceptional performance indefinitely is like expecting a sports star to never age or lose form.
Just as athletes have peak periods and declines, mutual funds can experience cycles of high and low performance.

Various factors, including market changes, economic shifts, and sector performance, can affect a fund's future returns.

It's important to remain realistic about expectations and understand that past performance, especially if exceptionally high, may not be sustainable indefinitely.

Neglecting to Consider Risk-Adjusted Returns When Evaluating Past Performance

Not considering risk-adjusted returns when evaluating a mutual fund's past performance is like measuring the speed of cars without considering their safety features.

A fund might show high returns, but if those returns come with high risk, it might not be the best choice for every investor.

Risk-adjusted returns consider the level of risk taken to achieve those returns, offering a more comprehensive view of the fund's performance.

A fund with lower returns but also lower risk might be a better option for some investors compared to a high-return, high-risk fund.

Understanding risk-adjusted returns helps in making more informed decisions that align with your risk tolerance and investment goals.

SELF-ASSESSMENT

Mutual Fund Past Performance Evaluation Questionnaire

I hope you have read the previous chapter carefully and I am sure some questions might be arising in your mind by now.

To find answers to those questions that are coming to your mind, and to decide whether you understand mutual fund past performance, you will find below a detailed questionnaire that will help you in making your decision.

The scoring points for these questionnaires are specified below:

Never	=	4
Rarely	=	3
Sometimes	=	2
Often	=	1
Always	=	0

QUESTION SET

1. Have you reviewed the mutual fund's performance over the past 5-10 years?

Answer: [   ]

2. Do you compare the fund's past performance with its benchmark index?

Answer: [   ]

3. How often do you check if the fund has consistently met or exceeded its performance goals?

Answer: [   ]

4. Do you evaluate how the fund performed during different market cycles (bull and bear markets)?

Answer: [   ]

5. How frequently do you assess the fund's performance in comparison to its peers?

Answer: [   ]

6. Do you investigate the reasons behind periods of underperformance or outperformance by the fund?

Answer: [   ]

7. How often do you review the fund manager's commentary on past performance?

Answer: [   ]

8. Do you consider the impact of fees on the fund's historical net performance?

Answer: [   ]

9. How regularly do you check for any changes in the fund's strategy that might affect past performance?

Answer: [   ]

10. Do you evaluate how the fund's risk level has contributed to its past performance?

Answer: [   ]

SCORING:

Total your points. A lower score suggests a thorough evaluation of the mutual fund's past performance, while a higher score indicates areas where deeper analysis may be beneficial before investing.

0-10 Points: Excellent assessment of past performance.

11-20 Points: Good review, but there may be certain aspects to examine more closely.

21-30 Points: Moderate evaluation; consider a more detailed analysis of past performance.

31-40 Points: Limited evaluation of past performance; in-depth review recommended before investing.

NOTES:

_____

_____

_____

_____

_____

_____

_____

6.
MARKET TIMING TRAPS

"Market Timing Traps" involve trying to predict the perfect moments to buy or sell in the stock market, which is highly risky and often ineffective.

It's like guessing when to jump on a fast-moving swing - more often than not, you might mistime it. This approach can lead to missing out on significant market gains if you sell too early or buy too late.

It also increases transaction costs and can lead to decisions driven by emotion rather than logic. Historically, attempting to time the market often results in lower returns compared to a steady, long-term investment strategy.

The safer bet is to invest consistently over time, riding out the market's ups and downs.

Ignoring the Challenges and Risks Associated with Market Timing

Overlooking the challenges and risks of market timing is like ignoring the danger signs on a treacherous road.

Market timing involves predicting when to buy or sell assets based on future market movements, but it's fraught with risks. The biggest challenge is the sheer unpredictability of the market.

Many factors, including economic data, geopolitical events, and investor sentiment, can affect market movements, and these are often impossible to predict accurately.

Mistiming the market, even by a small margin, can lead to significant losses or missed opportunities.

The risk of acting on inaccurate predictions often outweighs the potential benefits of successful market timing.

Failing to Distinguish Between Short-Term Volatility and Long-Term Trends

Not differentiating between short-term market volatility and long-term trends is like mistaking weather for climate.

Short-term volatility refers to quick and often unpredictable fluctuations in market prices, while long-term trends are more gradual and sustained movements over time.

Investors often react impulsively to short-term dips or spikes, mistaking these for lasting trends, which can lead to poor investment decisions.

Understanding that short-term volatility is a normal part of market behavior and focusing on the long-term trajectory can help maintain a more balanced and strategic investment approach.

Succumbing to the Fear of Missing Out (FOMO) in Market Timing

Giving in to FOMO in market timing is like rushing to join a party without knowing why everyone is there.

It's the anxiety that others are making profitable investments, leading you to make hasty, often ill-informed, decisions to buy or sell.

This fear can drive investors to jump into high-flying stocks or sectors without proper analysis, risking investments in overvalued assets or unsuitable ventures.

Avoiding FOMO requires a disciplined approach, adhering to your investment plan and goals, and resisting the urge to follow the crowd without a clear rationale.

Ignoring the Impact of Emotional Decision-Making on Market Timing

Neglecting the role of emotions in market timing decisions is like ignoring the influence of mood on impulse buying.

Emotions like fear, greed, and overconfidence can heavily influence investment decisions, particularly when trying to time the market.

Emotional responses to market ups and downs can lead to irrational decisions – selling in panic when markets dip or buying in euphoria during a surge.

These emotion-driven decisions often result in poor timing and investment choices. A more effective strategy involves setting a well-thought-out investment plan based on individual goals and risk tolerance and sticking to it regardless of short-term market movements.

Overtrading and Frequent Portfolio Turnover

Overtrading, or frequently buying and selling assets in your portfolio, is akin to a chef who constantly changes a recipe in the middle of cooking.

Each trade can incur transaction costs and taxes, which, when accumulated, can significantly eat into your returns.

High portfolio turnover might also indicate impulsive reactions to market movements rather than following a well-thought-out investment plan.

This frequent trading often fails to yield the expected benefits and can lead to lower overall performance due to the additional costs and potential short-term focus that overlooks longer-term opportunities.

Neglecting to Have a Disciplined Investment Strategy

Not having a disciplined investment strategy is like navigating without a map.

Without a clear plan, investing decisions might be influenced by market noise, trends, or emotions rather than a focused approach aligned with specific financial goals and risk tolerance.

A disciplined strategy involves setting clear objectives, choosing investments that align with these objectives, and sticking to this plan despite market fluctuations.

This approach helps in making informed decisions, avoiding impulsive reactions to market ups and downs, and maintaining a clear path toward your financial goals.

Failing to Rebalance a Portfolio in Response to Changing Market Conditions

Not rebalancing your portfolio considering changing market conditions is like not adjusting the sails of a boat when the wind changes direction.

Over time, the actual allocation of assets in your portfolio can drift away from your intended allocation due to varying performance across different assets.

Regular rebalancing – the process of buying or selling assets to maintain your desired asset allocation – ensures that your portfolio stays aligned with your risk tolerance and investment goals.

It also presents an opportunity to capitalize on market movements and systematic buying of assets at lower prices.

Ignoring the Potential Benefits of a Long-Term Buy-and-Hold Strategy

Overlooking the benefits of a long-term buy-and-hold strategy is like ignoring the virtues of patience in planting a garden.

This approach involves selecting high-quality investments and holding onto them over an extended period, allowing you to ride out market fluctuations and benefit from the compounding of returns.

It reduces the impact of short-term market volatility on your portfolio and often incurs lower transaction costs and taxes.

By staying invested over the long term, you give your investments ample time to grow and benefit from the overall upward trend of the markets.

SELF-ASSESSMENT

Market Timing Traps Understanding Questionnaire

I hope you have read the previous chapter carefully and I am sure some questions might be arising in your mind by now.

To find answers to those questions that are coming to your mind, and to decide whether you understand market timing traps, you will find below a detailed questionnaire that will help you in making your decision.

The scoring points for these questionnaires are specified below:

Never	=	4
Rarely	=	3
Sometimes	=	2
Often	=	1
Always	=	0

QUESTION SET

1. Do you try to predict short-term market movements before investing in a mutual fund?

Answer: [   ]

2. How often do you make investment decisions based on recent market trends or news?

Answer: [   ]

3. Do you consider the long-term performance of a mutual fund more important than short-term gains?

Answer: [   ]

4. How frequently do you change your investment strategy based on market fluctuations?

Answer: [   ]

5. Do you assess the risk of trying to time the market in terms of potential costs and missed opportunities?

Answer: [   ]

6. How often do you invest impulsively in reaction to a sudden market rise or fall?

Answer: [   ]

7. Do you understand the benefits of a long-term, consistent investment approach over trying to time the market?

Answer: [   ]

8. How regularly do you evaluate the performance of a mutual fund across different market cycles before investing?

Answer: [   ]

9. Do you consider the emotional biases that can influence market timing decisions?

Answer: [   ]

10. How often do you consult with a financial advisor to avoid the pitfalls of market timing?

Answer: [   ]

SCORING:

Add up your points. A lower score indicates a better understanding of the pitfalls of market timing, while a higher score suggests areas where further understanding and caution may be needed.

0-10 Points: Excellent grasp of market timing risks.

11-20 Points: Good awareness, but a more cautious approach is advised.

21-30 Points: Moderate understanding; further education recommended.

31-40 Points: Limited understanding; considerable risk of market timing traps.

NOTES:

_____
_____
_____
_____
_____
_____
_____

7.
FALLING FOR THE HOT NEW FUND

"Falling for the Hot New Fund" means investing in a new mutual fund just because it's popular or showing early high returns.

It's like buying a trendy product without checking if it suits your needs. These funds often lack a proven track record, making it hard to predict how they'll perform in the long run.

They might be doing well due to a current market trend, but this may not last. Also, new funds can carry higher risks and fees.

It's better to research thoroughly and consider how a fund fits into your overall investment strategy, rather than getting swayed by initial hype.

Investing in Funds Without a Proven Track Record

Investing in mutual funds without a proven track record is like buying a new car without checking its reviews or performance history.

A fund's track record provides important insights into its performance over different market conditions and periods.

New or unproven funds lack this historical data, making it difficult to assess their potential risks and returns.

While these funds might offer the allure of high returns or innovative strategies, they also come with uncertainty. Without a history to review, you're essentially taking a leap in the dark.

It's wise to consider funds with an established history that aligns with your investment goals and risk tolerance.

Falling for Market Hype and Media-Driven Investment Trends

Getting caught up in market hype and media-driven investment trends is like following a fashion trend without considering if it suits you.

The media often highlights funds that have recently performed well or are based on trending investment themes.

However, investing based on hype can lead to impulsive decisions, overlooking the fund's alignment with your investment strategy and risk tolerance.

Media attention can also inflate a fund's valuation, potentially leading to investments at peak prices.

It's important to base investment decisions on thorough research and analysis rather than media buzz.

Ignoring the Impact of High Demand on the Performance of Hot New Funds

Ignoring the impact of high investor demand on hot new funds is like overlooking the effect of overcrowding at a popular event.

When a new fund receives a lot of attention and investment, it can lead to an influx of capital.

While this might seem positive, it can pose challenges for the fund managers in effectively deploying the additional assets, especially in niche or limited markets.

This can dilute the fund's performance or lead to deviations from its core strategy. High demand can also drive up asset prices within the fund, affecting its value proposition.

It's important to consider the scalability of the fund's strategy and how increased assets under management could impact its performance.

Neglecting to Analyze the Underlying Assets and Strategy of Hot New Funds

Not examining the underlying assets and strategy of new, popular funds is like buying a house without inspecting its foundation.

These funds may be trending due to recent success or an innovative approach, but it's crucial to understand what they are investing in and how they plan to achieve their returns.

Look into the types of assets the fund holds, such as specific stocks, bonds, or sectors, and assess whether these align with current market trends and future potential.

Additionally, understand the fund's investment strategy - is it growth-oriented, value-focused, or income-generating? This analysis helps determine if the fund's approach is sound and sustainable and if it aligns with your investment objectives and risk tolerance.

Failing to Consider How Hot New Funds Fit into an Overall Portfolio

Investing in popular new funds without considering how they fit into your overall portfolio is like adding a piece to a puzzle without checking if it matches.

Each investment should have a clear role and purpose within your broader investment strategy.

Consider how the new fund complements or diversifies your existing portfolio. Does it add too much risk, or does it overlap with your current holdings?

The goal is to ensure that any new addition enhances your portfolio's diversification, aligns with your investment goals, and doesn't unnecessarily duplicate your existing investments.

Investing Based Solely on Recommendations from Friends or Family

Choosing to invest in a fund solely based on friends' or family members' recommendations is like wearing someone else's prescription glasses.

What works for one person may not suit another. Investment decisions should be based on your financial goals, risk tolerance, and research.

While recommendations can be a starting point, it's important to conduct your due diligence. Evaluate the fund's performance history, management team, investment strategy, and how it fits into your investment plan.

Relying solely on others' advice can lead to choices that aren't optimal for your unique financial situation.

Overlooking the Impact of Fees on the Returns of Hot New Funds

Ignoring the fees associated with new, popular funds is like overlooking the cost of maintaining a luxury car.

High fees can significantly eat into your returns, especially over the long term. Evaluate all fees associated with the fund, including management fees, performance fees, and any transaction costs.

Compare these fees with the fund's potential returns and other similar funds. Remember, higher fees require the fund to perform significantly better just to break even with lower-cost alternatives.

Always weigh the cost against the potential benefit.

Not Conducting Thorough Due Diligence Before Investing in New Funds

Failing to conduct thorough due diligence before investing in new funds is like signing a contract without reading the fine print.

Thorough research is crucial to understand the fund's potential risks and rewards. Examine the fund's prospectus, research the fund manager's track record and experience, and understand the fund's investment strategy in detail.

Look into the fund's performance in different market conditions and compare it with its peers.

Additionally, consider external factors such as market trends, economic outlook, and how the fund fits into your existing portfolio.

Comprehensive due diligence helps in making an informed investment decision and mitigates the risk of unpleasant surprises.

SELF-ASSESSMENT

Vulnerability to Hot New Fund Temptation

I hope you have read the previous chapter carefully and I am sure some questions might be arising in your mind by now.

To find answers to those questions that are coming to your mind, and to decide whether you are tempted to hot new funds in the market, you will find below a detailed questionnaire that will help you in making your decision.

The scoring points for these questionnaires are specified below:

Never   =   4
Rarely   =   3
Sometimes =   2
Often   =   1
Always   =   0

QUESTION SET

1. Do you often invest in a fund just because it has shown high returns recently?

Answer: [   ]

2. How frequently do you make investment decisions based on media hype or trends?

Answer: [   ]

3. Do you regularly research a fund's underlying assets and strategy before investing?

Answer: [   ]

4. How often do you consider how a new fund fits into your overall investment portfolio?

Answer: [   ]

5. Do you tend to invest in a fund because friends or family recommend it?

Answer: [   ]

6. How frequently do you evaluate the fees associated with a new fund before investing?

Answer: [   ]

7. Do you often find yourself attracted to investing in funds labeled as 'innovative' or 'breakthrough'?

Answer: [   ]

8. How often do you reassess your investment when a new fund becomes popular?

Answer: [   ]

9. Do you usually check the long-term performance history of a fund before investing?

Answer: [   ]

10. Are you likely to invest in a new fund without consulting a financial advisor?

Answer: [   ]

SCORING:

Total your points. A lower score indicates less likelihood of falling for the temptation of hot new funds, while a higher score suggests a greater propensity to be influenced by recent fund trends and media hype.

0-10 Points: Low susceptibility to hot new fund temptation.

11-20 Points: Moderate susceptibility; exercise caution and thorough research.

21-30 Points: High susceptibility; important to enhance due diligence.

31-40 Points: Very high susceptibility; critical to adopt a more disciplined investment approach.

NOTES:

_____

_____

_____

_____

_____

_____

8.
OVERLOOKING TAX IMPLICATIONS

"Overlooking Tax Implications" in mutual fund investing means not considering how taxes can impact your investment returns.

It's like forgetting to account for extra costs that can reduce your profits. When you earn money from mutual funds, through dividends or selling shares at a profit, these earnings can be taxed.

The type of fund, its turnover rate, and your tax bracket all affect how much tax you'll pay. Not thinking about these taxes can lead to smaller net returns than expected.

It's important to understand a fund's tax aspects, like how often it generates capital gains or the nature of its distributions, and plan your investment accordingly.

For more tax-efficient investing, consider the fund's tax features or use tax-advantaged accounts like IRAs.

Failing to Consider the Tax Implications of Investment Decisions

Not considering the tax implications when choosing mutual funds is like forgetting to factor in the cost of maintenance when buying a car.

Taxes can significantly affect your investment returns. Different types of investments are taxed differently.

For instance, dividends and interest income might be taxed at different rates, and the sale of fund shares can generate capital gains taxes.

Additionally, the turnover rate of a fund (how frequently its holdings are bought and sold) can also impact your tax liability. It's important to understand how your investments will be taxed and to factor this into your overall investment strategy.

This will help you estimate your actual, after-tax return and make more informed investment choices.

Ignoring the Impact of Capital Gains Taxes on Overall Returns

Overlooking capital gains taxes on mutual fund returns is like ignoring the cost of fuel when calculating a trip's expenses.

When you sell mutual fund shares for a profit, you may incur capital gains taxes. The rate of this tax depends on how long you held the investment (short-term vs. long-term capital gains).

These taxes can reduce your net returns, especially if you frequently buy and sell shares. Understanding the impact of capital gains taxes is crucial for accurately assessing the profitability of your investments.

It's important to factor in these taxes when calculating returns and to consider strategies that might minimize their impact, such as holding investments long-term.

Not Utilizing Tax-Efficient Investment Strategies

Not using tax-efficient investment strategies in mutual funds is like leaving money on the table.
Tax efficiency is about managing your investments in a way that minimizes the taxes you pay.

This can be achieved through strategies such as investing in funds with low turnover rates, which generate fewer taxable events, or choosing tax-efficient account types (like Roth IRAs or 401(k)s) for certain investments.

For taxable accounts, considering funds that are designed to be tax-efficient, such as index funds or ETFs, can be beneficial.

These strategies can help maximize your after-tax returns, making your investment efforts more fruitful.

Failing to Take Advantage of Tax-Advantaged Accounts

Not using tax-advantaged accounts for mutual fund investments is like missing out on legal ways to reduce your tax bill.

These accounts, such as IRAs (Individual Retirement Accounts) and 401(k)s, offer significant tax benefits.
For example, a traditional IRA may provide tax deductions on contributions and defer taxes on earnings until withdrawal, while a Roth IRA allows tax-free withdrawals under certain conditions.

Investing in mutual funds through these accounts can maximize your returns by minimizing the taxes paid.

It's a smart move to utilize these accounts to their fullest potential as part of your overall investment strategy, ensuring you're not paying more taxes than necessary on your investment gains.

Not Understanding the Tax Implications of Fund Distributions

Overlooking the tax implications of mutual fund distributions is like ignoring the extra costs on a utility bill.

Mutual funds often make distributions in the form of dividends or capital gains, and these can be taxable events. The way these distributions are taxed depends on various factors, such as the type of fund, the duration of your investment, and your tax bracket. Not understanding these aspects can lead to unexpected tax liabilities.

It's important to be aware of the potential tax consequences of your mutual fund's distributions to plan accordingly and avoid surprises come tax time.

Ignoring the Impact of Changes in Tax Laws on Investments

Ignoring changes in tax laws related to investments is like driving without keeping an eye on changing traffic signs.

Tax laws can change, and these changes can significantly impact the tax treatment of your investments.

Amendments in capital gains tax, dividend tax rates, or the rules governing retirement accounts can affect the after-tax returns of your mutual funds.

Staying informed about current tax laws and how they apply to your investments is crucial.

This knowledge allows you to make more informed decisions and possibly adjust your investment strategy to maintain its efficiency considering new tax rules.

Failing to Consult with a Tax Professional for Personalized Advice

Not consulting a tax professional for personalized advice on mutual fund investments is like trying to self-diagnose a medical condition without a doctor.

Tax professionals can provide tailored advice based on your specific financial situation, investment portfolio, and goals.

They can help you understand complex tax rules, identify tax-saving opportunities, and plan for tax-efficient investing.

Their expertise is especially valuable when dealing with complicated investment scenarios or significant changes in your financial life.

Seeking professional tax advice can ensure that your investment strategy is aligned with the most current tax laws and optimized for your tax situation.

Underestimating the Long-Term Impact of Taxes on Investment Returns

Underestimating the long-term impact of taxes on investment returns is like overlooking the effect of a small leak in a dam.

Over time, even a small reduction in your investment returns due to taxes can significantly erode the overall value of your portfolio.

Taxes can diminish your returns each year, and this loss compounds over time, reducing the amount of money available to grow.

Understanding the role of taxes and strategizing to minimize their impact is vital. This involves choosing tax-efficient funds, taking advantage of tax-advantaged accounts, and considering tax implications in your investment decisions.

Being mindful of taxes and planning accordingly can preserve more of your returns and enhance the growth of your investments in the long run.

SELF-ASSESSMENT

Tax Implications of Investment Decisions Questionnaire

I hope you have read the previous chapter carefully and I am sure some questions might be arising in your mind by now.

To find answers to those questions that are coming to your mind, and to decide whether you have considered tax implications before investing in Mutual Fund, you will find below a detailed questionnaire that will help you in making your decision.

The scoring points for these questionnaires are specified below:

Never	=	4
Rarely	=	3
Sometimes	=	2
Often	=	1
Always	=	0

QUESTION SET

1. Do you consider the tax consequences of mutual fund distributions (like dividends and capital gains) when investing?

Answer: [   ]

2. How often do you factor in the potential tax liability from selling mutual fund shares?

Answer: [   ]

3. Do you evaluate the tax efficiency of a mutual fund before investing?

Answer: [   ]

4. How frequently do you consider investing in tax-advantaged accounts like IRAs or 401(k)s for your mutual funds?

Answer: [   ]

5. Do you assess the impact of fund turnover on your tax situation?

Answer: [   ]

6. How often do you consult with a tax professional regarding your mutual fund investments?

Answer: [   ]

7. Do you consider the different tax treatments of various types of mutual funds (e.g., equity vs. bond funds)?

Answer: [   ]

8. How frequently do you review the tax implications of your mutual fund investments considering current tax laws?

Answer: [   ]

9. Do you consider the benefits of tax-loss harvesting when managing your mutual fund portfolio?

Answer: [   ]

10. Are you aware of and plan for state-specific tax implications on your mutual fund investments?

Answer: [   ]

SCORING:

Total your points. A lower score indicates a thorough consideration of tax implications in mutual fund investments, while a higher score suggests areas where more attention to tax factors may be beneficial.

0-10 Points: Excellent consideration of tax implications.

11-20 Points: Good awareness, but more focus on tax aspects may be helpful.

21-30 Points: Moderate awareness; further education on tax implications recommended.

31-40 Points: Limited consideration of tax implications; significant improvement needed.

NOTES:

_____

_____

_____

_____

_____

_____

_____

PART III:
DUE DILIGENCE IN FUND SELECTION

9.
RESEARCHING FUND MANAGERS

"Researching Fund Managers" means evaluating the person or team managing a mutual fund, much like checking a driver's record before getting into a car.

It involves looking at the fund manager's experience, how long they've been managing funds, and their performance history, especially during tough market conditions.

It's also important to understand their investment style – whether they're risk-takers or prefer a conservative approach, and if this aligns with your investment goals.

Stability matters too; frequent management changes can be a warning sign. Additionally, comparing their performance with similar funds gives you a sense of how skilled they are compared to their peers.

Essentially, a good fund manager can significantly influence a mutual fund's success, so evaluating their track record and approach is a crucial step in choosing the right fund.

Investing Without Understanding the Fund Manager's Philosophy and Strategy

Investing in a mutual fund without understanding the fund manager's philosophy and strategy is like setting sail without knowing the captain's plan.

The manager's approach to investing - whether they favor growth stocks, value stocks, or a mix, and their strategy for selecting these investments - is crucial.

This philosophy dictates how the fund is likely to perform under various market conditions. For example, a manager focusing on aggressive growth stocks might perform well in a bull market but could face significant risks in a downturn.

Understanding the manager's investment style helps ensure that the fund aligns with your investment goals and risk tolerance.

Neglecting to Assess the Manager's Track Record and Performance History

Not evaluating the fund manager's track record is like hiring an employee without reviewing their work history.

A manager's performance history provides insights into their skill, consistency, and ability to navigate different market environments.

Look at how the funds they've managed have performed over time, especially during market downturns. This historical performance, while not a guarantee of future results, can indicate the manager's expertise and decision-making skills.

A consistent track record of strong performance can be a good sign, while erratic or underwhelming results might be a red flag.

Not Considering the Manager's Tenure and Experience

Ignoring the fund manager's tenure and experience is akin to disregarding the experience of a pilot.

A manager with a long tenure likely has experience navigating various market cycles and economic conditions.

This experience can be invaluable, especially in challenging market environments. Managers who have been with a fund for only a short time may not have had the opportunity to fully implement their strategies or be tested by market volatility.

Longer tenure can also suggest stability in the fund's management approach.

Overemphasizing Short-Term Performance in Evaluating Fund Managers

Focusing too much on a fund manager's short-term performance is like judging a chef based on one meal.

Short-term results can be influenced by temporary market trends or anomalies and may not reflect the manager's overall skill and strategy.

It's more beneficial to look at longer-term performance, which can provide a clearer picture of the manager's ability to generate consistent returns.

This approach helps in understanding the manager's effectiveness over various market cycles, rather than basing judgments on potentially fleeting success.

Failing to Evaluate How Manager Changes May Impact Fund Performance

Not considering the impact of changes in fund management is like overlooking a change in a company's CEO.

A new manager can bring different strategies, philosophies, and risk preferences, which can significantly alter the fund's performance and alignment with its stated objectives.

It's important to assess the new manager's background, track record, and investment approach. Understand how these might differ from the previous manager and what changes might be expected in the fund's operation and performance.

A change in management should prompt a review of your investment to ensure it continues to meet your needs and expectations.

Falling for Star Fund Manager Allure Without Considering Team Dynamics

Being swayed by the allure of a 'star' fund manager without considering the dynamics of their team is like focusing on a lead singer while ignoring the band.

A single talented manager can be a draw, but the team supporting them is equally important. Investment management is often a collaborative effort, involving analysts and other experts.

A strong team can provide diverse perspectives and continuity if the lead manager leaves.

Assessing the team's collective experience, expertise, and stability is crucial in evaluating the fund's potential.

Not Considering How the Manager's Style Aligns with the Fund's Objectives

Ignoring whether a fund manager's style matches the fund's stated objectives is like expecting a sprinter to win a marathon.

Each manager has a unique style – some might focus on long-term growth, others on value, and some on income generation.

Ensure that this style aligns with the fund's objectives. For example, a manager who excels in aggressive growth strategies might not be suitable for a fund aimed at conservative income generation. Alignment between the manager's style and the fund's goals is key to meeting investment expectations.

Failing to Monitor Ongoing Performance and Managerial Changes

Not keeping track of a fund's ongoing performance and any changes in its management is like neglecting regular health check-ups.

Continuous monitoring is essential to ensure the fund remains on track to meet your investment goals.

Stay updated on the fund's performance relative to its peers and benchmarks. Additionally, be alert to any changes in the management team. A new manager can bring different strategies and risk profiles, potentially affecting the fund's performance.

Regular monitoring allows you to make informed decisions about whether to continue holding, sell, or adjust your investment in the fund.

SELF-ASSESSMENT

Fund Manager Research Assessment Questionnaire

I hope you have read the previous chapter carefully and I am sure some questions might be arising in your mind by now.

To find answers to those questions that are coming to your mind, and to decide whether you have researched Fund Manager before investing in Mutual Fund, you will find below a detailed questionnaire that will help you in making your decision.

The scoring points for these questionnaires are specified below:

Never	=	4
Rarely	=	3
Sometimes	=	2
Often	=	1
Always	=	0

QUESTION SET

1. Have you reviewed the fund manager's overall investment philosophy?

Answer: [   ]

2. Do you check the manager's track record with previous funds or investments?

Answer: [   ]

3. How often do you consider the fund manager's experience in the industry?

Answer: [   ]

4. Do you assess how long the manager has been with the specific fund?

Answer: [   ]

5. How frequently do you research the manager's performance during different market cycles?

Answer: [   ]

6. Do you evaluate the stability and expertise of the fund manager's supporting team?

Answer: [   ]

7. How often do you check if the manager invests their own money in the fund?

Answer: [   ]

8. Do you consider the alignment of the manager's compensation with fund performance?

Answer: [   ]

9. How regularly do you review any significant changes in the fund's management team?

Answer: [   ]

10. Are you aware of the manager's approach to risk and how it aligns with the fund's objectives?

Answer: [   ]

SCORING:

Total your points. A lower score indicates thorough research on the fund manager, while a higher score suggests areas where more in-depth investigation may be beneficial.

0-10 Points: Excellent understanding and research on fund managers.

11-20 Points: Good level of research, but some areas may need more attention.

21-30 Points: Moderate understanding; consider further research on fund managers.

31-40 Points: Limited understanding of fund managers; more comprehensive research is needed.

NOTES:

_____

_____

_____

_____

_____

_____

_____

10.
READING BETWEEN THE LINES: PROSPECTUS AND REPORTS

These are official documents to uncover essential details that might not be immediately obvious.

A prospectus and periodic reports contain crucial information about a fund's strategy, risks, fees, and past performance. However, key insights often lie in the finer details — like footnotes or the management discussion section.

For example, footnotes might reveal specific risks or how certain assets are valued, while management discussions can give a sense of the fund manager's outlook and strategy nuances.

Essentially, this careful examination goes beyond the surface to understand the fund's true nature and potential.

Overlooking Key Information Buried in the Footnotes of Reports

Ignoring information in the footnotes of mutual fund reports is like overlooking the fine print in a contract.

Footnotes often contain critical details about a fund's operations and investments. This can include specifics about holdings, methodologies for valuing assets, or additional explanations for performance metrics.

Overlooking this information can lead to an incomplete understanding of the fund's actual operations and potential risks.

Paying attention to footnotes can provide a fuller picture of the fund and help you make a more informed investment decision.

Not Paying Attention to the Fund's Investment Objectives and Policies

Not focusing on a mutual fund's investment objectives and policies is like setting off on a trip without a destination in mind.

These objectives and policies define the fund's goals and the strategies it will use to achieve them. They help you understand what the fund aims to accomplish and how it plans to get there, such as focusing on long-term growth, income generation, or capital preservation.

Knowing these objectives and policies is crucial to assess whether the fund meets your own investment goals and risk profile.

Ignoring the Risks and Limitations Outlined in the Prospectus

Overlooking the risks and limitations outlined in a mutual fund's prospectus is like ignoring safety warnings on a product.

Every investment carries certain risks, and mutual funds are no exception. The prospectus provides detailed information about these risks, including market risk, credit risk, and liquidity risk.

It also outlines any limitations or restrictions on the fund's operations. Understanding these risks and limitations is vital to making an informed decision and selecting a fund that fits within your comfort zone in terms of risk exposure.

Neglecting to Scrutinize Fund Expenses and Fees in the Reports

Overlooking the expenses and fees detailed in mutual fund reports is like ignoring the fine print in a billing statement.

These costs, such as management fees, transaction fees, and other operational expenses, directly impact your investment returns.

Even small differences in fees can significantly affect your returns over time due to the compounding effect. It's crucial to understand all associated costs of a fund, as they vary significantly across funds and can erode your investment gains.

By carefully examining these fees, you can make more cost-effective choices and ensure that your investment grows efficiently.

Relying Solely on Rating Agencies Without Reading Fund Documents

Depending solely on ratings from agencies without examining the fund's documents is like buying a product based only on online reviews without checking its specifications.

Ratings provide a quick overview of a fund's past performance and quality, but they don't tell the whole story. They are based on historical data and may not reflect current or future performance.

Reading the fund's prospectus and annual reports gives you a deeper insight into its investment strategy, risks, management style, and other crucial details.

This comprehensive understanding is essential for making an informed investment decision.

Disregarding the Importance of Shareholder Reports and Updates

Ignoring shareholder reports and regular updates from a mutual fund is like not reading important letters from a business partner.

These reports offer valuable insights into the fund's performance, changes in its portfolio, and the fund manager's outlook and strategy.

They also provide context on how market conditions affect the fund. Regularly reviewing these updates helps you stay informed about the fund's health and any shifts that might impact its performance.

This information is vital for evaluating whether the fund continues to meet your investment objectives.

Failing to Compare Fund Documents Across Similar Investment Options

Not comparing documents of similar mutual funds is like shopping without comparing products from different brands.

Just as you would compare features and prices of similar items, it's important to compare the prospectuses and annual reports of similar funds.

Look at aspects like investment strategies, performance history, fees, and risk profiles. This comparison helps you understand the relative merits and drawbacks of each option, ensuring that you choose a fund that best suits your investment goals and risk appetite.

Not Seeking Professional Advice When Interpreting Complex Fund Documents

Avoiding professional advice for interpreting complex mutual fund documents is like avoiding expert consultation for a major health decision.

Financial professionals can help demystify the jargon, clarify complex investment strategies, and explain the implications of fees and fund policies.

Their expertise is particularly valuable for understanding sophisticated or high-stakes investments.

A financial advisor can guide you through the nuances of fund documents, ensuring that you fully understand the investment you are considering and how it fits into your overall financial plan.

SELF-ASSESSMENT

Mutual Fund Prospectus and Reports Review Questionnaire

I hope you have read the previous chapter carefully and I am sure some questions might be arising in your mind by now.

To find answers to those questions that are coming to your mind, and to decide whether you have read the company prospectus and reports before investing in Mutual Fund, you will find below a detailed questionnaire that will help you in making your decision.

The scoring points for these questionnaires are specified below:

Never	=	4
Rarely	=	3
Sometimes	=	2
Often	=	1
Always	=	0

QUESTION SET

1. Do you read the prospectus of a mutual fund before investing in it?

Answer: [   ]

2. How often do you review the fund's annual and semi-annual reports?

Answer: [   ]

3. Do you regularly check the fund manager's commentary in the reports?

Answer: [   ]

4. How frequently do you scrutinize the fee structure as outlined in the prospectus?

Answer: [   ]

5. Do you assess the investment strategy and objectives detailed in the prospectus?

Answer: [   ]

6. How often do you review the risk disclosures in the prospectus?

Answer: [   ]

7. Do you compare the information in the prospectus with other similar mutual funds?

Answer: [   ]

8. How regularly do you check for updates or amendments to the prospectus?

Answer: [   ]

9. Do you pay attention to the historical performance data included in the reports?

Answer: [   ]

10. Are you aware of the specific holdings and sector allocations detailed in the fund reports?

Answer: [   ]

SCORING:

Total your points. A lower score indicates thorough research and understanding of the mutual fund through its prospectus and reports, while a higher score suggests areas where increased attention may be beneficial.

0-10 Points: Excellent comprehension of the fund's documentation.

11-20 Points: Good understanding, but some aspects might require closer review.

21-30 Points: Moderate awareness; further detailed review recommended.

31-40 Points: Limited engagement with fund documentation; substantial review needed.

NOTES:

_____

_____

_____

_____

_____

_____

PART IV: ADVANCED STRATEGIES FOR SUCCESS

11.
TACTICAL ASSET ALLOCATION

This strategy is used in mutual fund investing where you temporarily adjust your investment mix to capitalize on specific market opportunities or to dodge potential risks.

It's like a soccer coach making strategic player changes during a game to respond to the opposing team's tactics.

Normally, you might have a set investment plan based on your long-term goals. However, with tactical asset allocation, you make short-term shifts in your assets — like moving more into stocks or bonds based on current market conditions.

This approach aims to enhance returns or reduce risk in response to changing market trends, but it requires careful market analysis and timing.

Neglecting the Benefits of Adapting to Changing Market Conditions

Overlooking the need to adapt to changing market conditions is like using an old map for a rapidly developing city.

Markets evolve, and sticking rigidly to an initial investment strategy without considering these changes can lead to missed opportunities or increased risks.

For example, a booming sector may become overvalued, or a once-stagnant market might start showing growth potential. Regularly assessing the market's current state allows for adjustments in your investment strategy, ensuring it remains aligned with both current conditions and your long-term goals.

Adaptation might involve shifting focus among asset classes, sectors, or geographical regions based on prevailing market trends and forecasts.

Failing to Reassess and Adjust Asset Allocation Over Time

Not reassessing and adjusting your asset allocation over time is akin to wearing the same clothes regardless of the changing seasons.

As time passes, your financial situation, goals, and risk tolerance can change, and so should your asset allocation.

For instance, as you approach retirement, you might want to shift from growth-oriented investments to more conservative, income-generating assets.

Regularly reviewing and adjusting your asset allocation helps ensure that your portfolio continues to reflect your current needs, goals, and risk appetite.

Not Having a Systematic Approach to Tactical Asset Allocation

Lacking a systematic approach to tactical asset allocation is like sailing without a compass.

Tactical asset allocation involves making short-term adjustments to your investment portfolio to capitalize on market opportunities or mitigate risks.

Without a clear, methodical approach, these adjustments can be haphazard and ineffective. A systematic strategy should be based on thorough research, clear criteria for making changes, and a disciplined process for implementing them.

This approach ensures that any tactical moves are well-considered and contribute positively to your overall investment strategy.

Ignoring the Impact of Economic Indicators on Asset Allocation Decisions

Ignoring economic indicators when making asset allocation decisions is like driving without paying attention to road signs.

Economic indicators, such as interest rates, inflation, GDP growth, and employment figures, provide crucial insights into the overall health of the economy and potential market trends.

These indicators can signal the need for adjustments in your asset allocation. For example, rising interest rates might make bond investments less attractive, while strong GDP growth could signal a favorable environment for equities.

Staying informed about economic trends helps in making more informed asset allocation decisions.

Reacting Impulsively to Short-Term Market Fluctuations

Reacting impulsively to short-term market fluctuations is like changing your travel plans at every turn in the weather.

While markets can be volatile in the short term, making hasty decisions based on these fluctuations can harm your long-term investment goals.

It's essential to distinguish between short-term noise and fundamental changes in the market. A well-thought-out investment strategy considers your long-term objectives and tolerates some degree of short-term volatility.

Avoid making impulsive decisions based on temporary market movements, as they can derail a well-planned investment strategy.

Underestimating the Importance of Rebalancing in Asset Allocation

Not giving due importance to rebalancing your asset allocation is like neglecting regular maintenance of your vehicle.

Over time, the initial allocation of your investments can drift due to the varying performance of different assets.

For instance, a strong stock market performance might increase the percentage of stocks in your portfolio, exposing you to more risk than intended.

Rebalancing involves adjusting your holdings back to their original allocation, ensuring they continue to align with your risk tolerance and investment goals.
This practice not only maintains the desired risk level but also systematically prompts you to buy low and sell high, optimizing your portfolio's performance over the long term.

Ignoring the Role of Market Trends in Tactical Asset Allocation

Disregarding the role of market trends in tactical asset allocation is like driving without observing road signs.

Market trends, whether short-term or long-term, provide valuable cues for making tactical adjustments in your investment portfolio.

By recognizing these trends, you can make informed decisions to temporarily increase or decrease exposure to certain asset classes or sectors.

For example, during a bullish trend in technology stocks, you might increase your tech holdings.

However, it's crucial to maintain a balance and ensure these adjustments align with your overall investment strategy and risk tolerance.

Overemphasizing Short-term Tactical Moves at the Expense of Long-term Strategy

Focusing too much on short-term tactical moves in your investment strategy is like being overly concerned with the day's weather while neglecting the climate trend.

While tactical asset allocation can capitalize on short-term opportunities, it should not overshadow your long-term investment strategy.

Excessive trading and frequent changes in response to short-term market movements can lead to higher transaction costs, tax implications, and potential misalignment with your fundamental investment objectives.

It's essential to keep these tactical moves within the broader context of your long-term financial goals, ensuring they complement rather than detract from your overall strategy.

SELF-ASSESSMENT

Tactical Asset Allocation Understanding Questionnaire

I hope you have read the previous chapter carefully and I am sure some questions might be arising in your mind by now.

To find answers to those questions that are coming to your mind, and to decide whether you understand the tactical allocation of Mutual Funds before investing in it, you will find below a detailed questionnaire that will help you in making your decision.

The scoring points for these questionnaires are specified below:

Never	=	4
Rarely	=	3
Sometimes	=	2
Often	=	1
Always	=	0

QUESTION SET

1. Do you understand the concept of tactical asset allocation and its purpose?

Answer: [   ]

2. How often do you adjust your asset allocation in response to short-term market trends?

Answer: [   ]

3. Do you consider how tactical adjustments fit into your overall long-term investment strategy?

Answer: [   ]

4. How frequently do you assess market trends and economic indicators for tactical asset allocation?

Answer: [   ]

5. Do you review and adjust your investment portfolio based on tactical asset allocation principles regularly?

Answer: [   ]

6. How often do you consider the tax implications of making tactical asset allocation changes?

Answer: [   ]

7. Do you evaluate the transaction costs associated with frequent adjustments in your asset allocation?

Answer: [   ]

8. How frequently do you reassess your risk tolerance in line with tactical asset allocation decisions?

Answer: [   ]

9. Do you stay informed about different asset classes and sectors for effective tactical asset allocation?

Answer: [   ]

10. Are you aware of and do you plan for the potential short-term and long-term impacts of tactical asset allocation on your portfolio?

Answer: [   ]

SCORING:

Total your points. A lower score indicates a solid understanding of tactical asset allocation, while a higher score suggests areas where more learning or consultation may be beneficial.

0-10 Points: Excellent grasp of tactical asset allocation principles.

11-20 Points: Good understanding, but some aspects might need further exploration.

21-30 Points: Moderate understanding; additional education on tactical allocation recommended.

31-40 Points: Limited understanding; significant improvement needed in understanding tactical asset allocation.

NOTES:

_____

_____

_____

_____

_____

_____

12.
THE ROLE OF INDEX FUNDS AND ETFS

It is like having a dependable, low-maintenance vehicle in your investment garage. Index funds and ETFs (Exchange-Traded Funds) are designed to track the performance of a specific market index, like the S&P 500.

They offer a straightforward and cost-effective way to invest in a broad swath of the market. This makes them great tools for diversification, reducing the risk that comes from betting on individual stocks.

Index funds are known for their lower fees compared to actively managed funds, while ETFs add the flexibility of being traded like stocks.

Both are excellent options for investors looking for market exposure without the complexity of picking individual stocks.

Ignoring the Benefits of Passive Investing with Index Funds

Overlooking the advantages of passive investing through index funds is like ignoring a steady and reliable path in favor of a more uncertain one.

Index funds aim to replicate the performance of a specific market index, such as the S&P 500.

They offer a low-cost, straightforward way to invest in a broad section of the market. These funds are typically more cost-efficient than actively managed funds since they don't require the same level of active decision-making or research.

By investing in index funds, you get a diversified portfolio that mirrors the performance of the selected index, often leading to more predictable outcomes and lower fees.

This makes them an appealing choice for long-term investors seeking steady market exposure.

Failing to Understand the Differences Between Index Funds and Actively Managed Funds

Not recognizing the key differences between index funds and actively managed funds is like confusing two distinct financial tools.

Index funds are designed to passively track the performance of a specific index, thereby reflecting the market's overall movement.

In contrast, actively managed funds are managed by fund managers who actively select investments, aiming for higher returns than their benchmark indexes.

Active management often incurs higher fees due to the involved research and active trading. Understanding these differences is crucial as they affect your investment approach, potential returns, and costs.

Index funds offer simplicity and lower fees, while actively managed funds aim for higher returns, albeit with higher risks and costs.

Overlooking the Cost Advantages of Index Funds and ETFs

Ignoring the cost advantages of index funds and ETFs (Exchange-Traded Funds) is like overlooking a more economical option for a similar product.

These funds typically have lower expense ratios compared to actively managed funds. This is because they are passively managed and mirror a market index, requiring less research and fewer transactions.

Lower fees mean that more of your investment stays invested and can grow over time. Additionally, ETFs often offer greater tax efficiency due to their unique structure.

For investors conscious of investment costs and seeking market-average returns, index funds and ETFs can be an attractive option.

Underestimating the Potential Benefits of Broad Market Exposure

Underestimating the benefits of broad market exposure offered by index funds is like not recognizing the value of a diversified investment.

Index funds provide an easy way to invest across a wide range of stocks or bonds, representing an entire index.

This broad market exposure helps in diversifying your investment, reducing the risk that comes from investing in individual stocks or sectors.

For long-term investors, this diversification can lead to more stable returns, mirroring the overall market's growth.

Broad market exposure is particularly beneficial for those seeking to invest in line with market trends without the need to analyze individual stocks extensively.

Neglecting to Use Index Funds as Core Holdings in a Diversified Portfolio

Not including index funds as core holdings in a diversified portfolio is like building a house without a solid foundation.

Index funds provide broad market exposure, replicating the performance of a market index like the S&P 500.

They offer a low-cost, effective way to achieve diversification, reducing the risk that comes from concentrating investments in individual stocks or sectors.

By making index funds a central part of your portfolio, you can capture the general market's returns, which is often sufficient for most investors.

This strategy is especially beneficial for long-term investors who want a stable, hands-off approach to investing.

Failing to Recognize the Limitations of Index Investing

Overlooking the limitations of index investing is like assuming a one-size-fits-all solution for different financial goals.

While index funds offer broad market exposure and cost efficiency, they also have limitations. They are designed to match, not outperform, the market index.

This means in a declining market, index funds will also decline in value. Additionally, they may not offer the flexibility to avoid specific risks or to capitalize on unique market opportunities.

Understanding these limitations is important for investors who might be seeking more than average market returns or who have specific investment goals that require a more tailored approach.

Not Diversifying Across Different Index Funds for Added Exposure

Not diversifying across various index funds is like limiting your diet to only one food group.

Just as nutritional balance is achieved through a variety of foods, investment balance is achieved through diversifying across different index funds.

Different index funds track different segments of the market, such as large-cap stocks, small-cap stocks, international stocks, or bonds.

By diversifying across these different index funds, you can achieve broader market exposure and balance your portfolio's risk.

This approach helps mitigate the impact of volatility in any one market segment on your overall portfolio.

Disregarding the Impact of Market Conditions on the Performance of Index Funds

Ignoring how market conditions affect index funds is like overlooking weather forecasts when planning an outdoor event.

Index funds mirror the performance of their respective indices, which means they are directly impacted by overall market conditions.

In a bull market, index funds will generally perform well, while in a bear market, their value may decline.

Investors need to understand that investing in index funds involves experiencing the highs and lows of the market. Being aware of this can help in setting realistic expectations and not being swayed by short-term market fluctuations.

SELF-ASSESSMENT

Understanding Index Funds and ETFs Questionnaire

I hope you have read the previous chapter carefully and I am sure some questions might be arising in your mind by now.

To find answers to those questions that are coming to your mind, and to decide whether you understand the Index Funds and ETFs, you will find below a detailed questionnaire that will help you in making your decision.

The scoring points for these questionnaires are specified below:

Never	=	4
Rarely	=	3
Sometimes	=	2
Often	=	1
Always	=	0

QUESTION SET

1. Do you understand the basic concept of what an index fund is and how it works?

Answer: [   ]

2. How often do you compare the performance of index funds with actively managed funds?

Answer: [   ]

3. Do you recognize the difference between index funds and Exchange-Traded Funds (ETFs)?

Answer: [   ]

4. How frequently do you consider index funds or ETFs for their cost-efficiency in terms of fees and expenses?

Answer: [   ]

5. Do you evaluate the diversification benefits of index funds or ETFs in your portfolio?

Answer: [   ]

6. How often do you assess the tax efficiency of index funds and ETFs for your investment portfolio?

Answer: [   ]

7. Do you consider the potential tracking error in index funds compared to their benchmark indices?

Answer: [   ]

8. How frequently do you research the liquidity of ETFs before investing in them?

Answer: [   ]

9. Do you consider the market exposure provided by index funds and ETFs in your investment decisions?

Answer: [   ]

10. Are you aware of the potential for passive investing strategies, like index funds and ETFs, in long-term wealth accumulation?

Answer: [   ]

SCORING:

Total your points. A lower score indicates a strong understanding of Index Funds and ETFs, while a higher score suggests areas where more learning may be beneficial.

0-10 Points: Excellent grasp of the role and function of Index Funds and ETFs.

11-20 Points: Good understanding, but some areas might need more in-depth exploration.

21-30 Points: Moderate understanding; further education on Index Funds and ETFs recommended.

31-40 Points: Limited understanding; significant learning needed in this area.

NOTES:

_____

_____

_____

_____

_____

_____

_____

13.
DOLLAR-COST AVERAGING

This involves regularly investing a fixed amount of money over time, regardless of the market's ups and downs.

It's like steadily adding water to a bucket during both rain and sunshine. By investing a set amount at regular intervals, say monthly, you buy more shares when prices are low and fewer when prices are high.

This approach can help reduce the impact of market volatility on your investment and lower the risk of investing a large amount at the wrong time.

Over time, dollar-cost averaging can lead to a lower average cost per share, making it a simple yet effective strategy for long-term investors.

Ignoring the Benefits of Consistent, Disciplined Investing

Overlooking the benefits of consistent, disciplined investing is like ignoring the power of steady progress in achieving long-term goals.

Regular and disciplined investing, particularly in mutual funds, helps in smoothing out the risks associated with market volatility.

It's like a steady journey towards a destination, rather than a series of erratic sprints. By investing consistently, you reduce the temptation to time the market and potentially miss out on valuable growth opportunities.

This approach allows your investments to compound over time, which can significantly increase your potential returns in the long run.

Failing to Implement a Systematic Approach to Dollar-Cost Averaging

Not using a systematic approach to dollar-cost averaging is like sailing without a compass.

Dollar-cost averaging involves regularly investing a fixed amount of money, which can help mitigate the risk of market fluctuations.

By neglecting this strategy, you might make hasty decisions based on short-term market movements, potentially buying high and selling low.

A systematic approach ensures you purchase more shares when prices are low and fewer when prices are high, which can lead to a lower average cost per share over time.

It's a disciplined strategy that can be particularly effective in volatile markets.

Reacting Emotionally to Short-Term Market Fluctuations During Dollar-Cost Averaging

Responding emotionally to short-term market fluctuations while practicing dollar-cost averaging is like changing course in response to every wind gust while sailing.

The essence of dollar-cost averaging is to invest a fixed amount regularly regardless of market conditions, thereby averaging out the cost of investment.

Emotional reactions, such as panic selling or exuberant buying, can undermine this strategy.

It's important to stay committed to your regular investment schedule, irrespective of short-term market movements, to fully benefit from this approach.

Neglecting to Reassess and Adjust the Dollar-Cost Averaging Strategy Over Time

Failing to periodically reassess and adjust your dollar-cost averaging strategy is like not recalibrating your navigation system for current conditions.

Over time, your financial situation, market conditions, and investment goals may change.

Sticking rigidly to an initial dollar-cost averaging plan without considering these changes can lead to suboptimal investment outcomes.

Periodically reviewing and adjusting your investment amount or the funds you are investing in ensures that your strategy remains aligned with your current goals and market opportunities.

Not Taking Advantage of Market Downturns to Increase Investment Positions

Not leveraging market downturns to increase investment positions overlooks a key opportunity in investment strategy.

Market dips provide a chance to purchase more shares at lower prices, potentially increasing your long-term returns.

By not adjusting your investment strategy during these times, you may miss out on the chance to 'buy low'.

If your financial situation allows, increasing your investment during downturns can be a strategic move to capitalize on lower market prices, aligning with the principle of buying low and selling high.

Underestimating the Impact of Compounding Through Consistent Investments

Not fully appreciating the power of compounding in consistent investments is like ignoring the snowball effect.

Compounding is the process where the earnings from an investment generate their earnings over time.

By regularly investing in a mutual fund and reinvesting the returns, the compound effect can significantly boost the growth of your investment.

This growth accelerates over time, as the returns on your original investment, along with the returns on your reinvested earnings, all start to generate more returns.

Therefore, underestimating compounding can mean missing out on the substantial growth potential that consistent, long-term investments offer.

Ignoring the Long-Term Benefits of a Dollar-Cost Averaging Approach

Overlooking the long-term benefits of dollar-cost averaging is like not seeing the forest for the trees.

Dollar-cost averaging involves regularly investing a fixed amount of money, regardless of market fluctuations.

This strategy can reduce the impact of short-term market volatility on your investment. Over time, as you consistently invest, this approach can help average out the cost of your mutual fund shares, potentially lowering the average cost per share compared to making a lump-sum investment.

By ignoring this strategy, you might miss out on a disciplined, systematic way of investing that can potentially lead to better long-term results.

Not Communicating and Aligning Dollar-Cost Averaging Strategy with Overall Financial Goals

Failing to align your dollar-cost averaging strategy with your overall financial goals is akin to walking without a destination.

Your investment strategy should be a part of a larger financial plan that includes your short-term and long-term goals, such as retirement, buying a home, or funding education.

Without aligning your regular investment approach with these objectives, you might either fall short of your goals or take on more risk than necessary.

It's important to periodically review your financial goals and adjust your investment strategy, accordingly, ensuring that your regular investments are effectively contributing to achieving your broader financial aspirations.

CONCLUSION

Now we are at the end of the book. So, let's understand the conclusion and key takeaways about what we have discussed in previous chapters.

Importance of Long-Term Planning and Commitment

The key to successful mutual fund investing lies in long-term planning and commitment. This approach is like cultivating a garden; it requires patience, regular care, and time for the seeds to grow into fruitful plants.

When you invest with a long-term perspective, you allow your investments the time they need to overcome market fluctuations and benefit from the potential of compounding returns.

This strategy also helps in mitigating the risk of making impulsive decisions based on short-term market movements.

Long-term planning involves setting clear financial goals, such as retirement savings, children's education, or building wealth, and sticking to a consistent investment plan to achieve these objectives.

A committed approach, coupled with regular monitoring and rebalancing, ensures that your investment journey stays on track, even amidst the ups and downs of the market.

Remember, successful investing is not about timing the market; it's about time in the market.

Developing a Personalized Investment Strategy

Creating a personalized investment strategy is essential for effective mutual fund investing. This process involves tailoring your investment approach to fit your unique financial situation, goals, risk tolerance, and time horizon.

It's like getting a custom-made suit; it fits you perfectly and suits your individual needs. Start by assessing your financial situation, including your income, expenses, debts, and savings.

Then, define your investment goals – whether it's saving for retirement, a down payment on a house, or your child's education.

Your risk tolerance – how much risk you are willing and able to take – and your investment time frame – how long you plan to invest – are crucial in determining the right mix of funds for your portfolio.

A personalized strategy ensures that your investments are aligned with your personal financial goals, making it more likely that you'll stay committed and comfortable with your investment choices over the long haul.

Staying Informed and Adapting to Changing Market Conditions

Keeping informed and adapting to changing market conditions is crucial in managing a successful mutual fund portfolio.

The financial market is dynamic, much like a shifting weather pattern. Being informed means regularly keeping up with financial news, market trends, and economic indicators that can influence your investments.

However, staying informed doesn't imply reacting to every market fluctuation. It's about understanding the bigger picture and making educated decisions. Flexibility in your investment approach is also key.

This could mean adjusting your asset allocation in response to significant economic shifts or rebalancing your portfolio to maintain your desired risk level.

Staying informed and adaptable helps you navigate through the complexities of the market, ensuring your investment strategy remains relevant and effective.

Building a Successful and Sustainable Mutual Fund Portfolio

Building a successful and sustainable mutual fund portfolio is like constructing a well-balanced and sturdy building.

It requires a foundation of clear goals and a mix of investments that aligns with your risk tolerance and time horizon.

Diversification is the cornerstone of a good portfolio. This means spreading your investments across different asset classes (stocks, bonds, etc.), sectors, and geographical regions to reduce risk.

Regularly reviewing and rebalancing your portfolio is also crucial. This ensures that your investments stay aligned with your goals and adapt to any changes in your life or financial circumstances.

Remember, a well-planned and diversified portfolio increases your chances of weathering market volatility and achieving long-term financial success.

THANK YOU!

www.ingramcontent.com/pod-product-compliance
Lightning Source LLC
Chambersburg PA
CBHW030446290526
45786CB00001B/473